S0-BRQ-913

HOUGHTON MIFFLIN

Georgia
Science

HOUGHTON MIFFLIN   BOSTON

Program Authors

William Badders
Director of the Cleveland Mathematics and Science Partnership
Cleveland Municipal School District, Cleveland, Ohio

Douglas Carnine, Ph.D.
Professor of Education
University of Oregon, Eugene, Oregon

Bobby Jeanpierre, Ph.D.
Assistant Professor, Science Education
University of Central Florida, Orlando, Florida

James Feliciani
Supervisor of Instructional Media and Technology
Land O' Lakes, Florida

Carolyn Sumners, Ph.D.
Director of Astronomy and Physical Sciences
Houston Museum of Natural Science, Houston, Texas

Catherine Valentino
Author-in-Residence
Houghton Mifflin, West Kingston, Rhode Island

Content Consultants

See Teacher's Edition for a complete list.

Copyright © 2009 by Houghton Mifflin Company. All rights reserved.

No part of this work may be reproduced or transmitted in any form or by any means, electronic or mechanical, including photocopying or recording, or by any information storage or retrieval system without prior written permission of Houghton Mifflin Company unless such copying is expressly permitted by federal copyright law. Address inquiries to School Permissions, Houghton Mifflin Company, 222 Berkeley St., Boston, MA 02116.

Printed in the U.S.A.

ISBN 13: 978-0-618-88488-9
ISBN 10: 0-618-88488-2

4 5 6 7 8 9-DSV-16 15 14 13 12 11 10 09 08

Georgia Teacher Reviewers

Peggy Baugh
Douglas County Board of Education
Douglasville, Georgia

Douglas O. Carroll
White Bluff Elementary
Savannah, Georgia

Vanessa Hooks Denison
Garden City Elementary
Garden City, Georgia

Theresa Drago
Collins Elementary School
Augusta, Georgia

Kimberly Geralds
Settles Bridge Elementary
Suwanee, Georgia

Amy R. Hillman
Freedom Park Elementary
Augusta, Georgia

Lisa Iennaccaro-Hills
Chattahoochee Elementary
Cumming, Georgia

Megan Horsley
Sawnee Primary School
Cumming, Georgia

Marsha Mattson
Bascomb Elementary
Woodstock, Georgia

Janyce Moreland
Emma Hutchinson Elementary
Atlanta, Georgia

Roxanne Peterson
Pine Street Elementary
Conyers, Georgia

Barbara Ramps
Liberty Elementary
Midway, Georgia

James Roszkowiak
Spencer Elementary
Savannah, Georgia

Donna Smith
Russell Elementary
Smyrna, Georgia

Debbie Wallace
Sawnee Primary School
Cumming, Georgia

Contents

UNIT A
Earth Science

Big Idea Weather patterns can be observed, measured, and described.

every step you make
something moves.

Piedmont Park, Atlanta

Contents

UNIT B
Physical Science

Big Idea Light and sound can be observed and measured. The effects of magnets can also be observed.

Reed Bingham State Park, Georgia

Contents

UNIT C
Life Science

Big Idea Plants and animals meet their needs in different ways.

Features

Inquiry Focus Activities

. . . stimulates children's critical thinking and research skills. Children will take opportunities presented to ask questions they are pondering and seek to create new meaning from their experiences with the activities listed here.

EARTH A SCIENCE

PHYSICAL UNIT B SCIENCE

LIFE UNIT C SCIENCE

Georgia Science

Using Your Book

The Nature of Science

In the front of your book you will learn about how people explore science.

Every unit in your book has two or more chapters.

The Nature of Science

59

Big Idea! tells you the science idea that connects the content of each lesson.

Independent Books You can read these on your own.

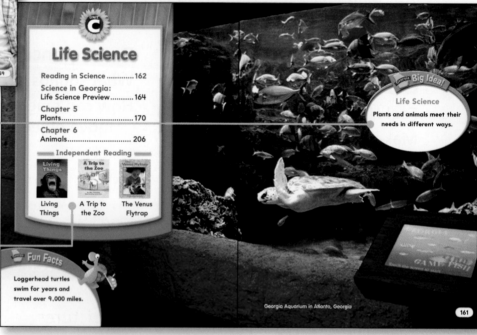

UNIT C

Life Science

Independent Reading

Living Things | A Trip to the Zoo | The Venus Flytrap

Big Idea!

Life Science

Plants and animals meet their needs in different ways.

Fun Facts

Loggerhead turtles swim for years and travel over 9,000 miles.

Georgia Aquarium in Atlanta, Georgia

161

Every unit begins with a special Science in Georgia feature.

Science in Georgia

STANDARDS S1E1a. Identify different types of weather and the characteristics of each type.

What Is Weather Like in Georgia?

Summer Weather?

Hot and sticky! How do you cool off?

17° below zero!
January 27, 1940 was Georgia's coldest day ever.

112°
July 24, 1953 was Georgia's hottest day ever.

Floyd County · Atlanta
Louisville

GEORGIA

4 • Unit A

5

Lesson Preview gives information and asks questions about each lesson.

Chapter 5

Plants

Lesson Preview

LESSON 1 Strawberries are plants. What do plants need to grow?

LESSON 2 Buttercups have flowers and leaves. What are other plant parts?

LESSON 3 A plant's roots are below the ground. What do roots do?

LESSON 4 Leaves grow toward light. Why does this happen?

170   171

Vocabulary Preview

Introduces important science terms with pictures and vocabulary skills.

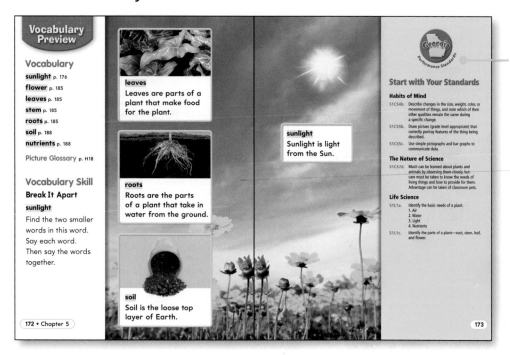

Vocabulary Preview

Vocabulary

sunlight p. 176
flower p. 185
leaves p. 185
stem p. 185
roots p. 185
soil p. 188
nutrients p. 188

Picture Glossary p. H18

Vocabulary Skill

Break It Apart
sunlight
Find the two smaller words in this word. Say each word. Then say the words together.

leaves
Leaves are parts of a plant that make food for the plant.

roots
Roots are the parts of a plant that take in water from the ground.

soil
Soil is the loose top layer of Earth.

sunlight
Sunlight is light from the Sun.

Start with Your Standards

Habits of Mind

S1CS4b. Describe changes in the size, weight, color, or movement of things, and note which of their other qualities remain the same during a specific change.

S1CS5b. Draw pictures (grade level appropriate) that correctly portray features of the thing being described.

S1CS5c. Use simple pictographs and bar graphs to communicate data.

The Nature of Science

S1CS7d. Much can be learned about plants and animals by observing them closely, but care must be taken to know the needs of living things and how to provide for them. Advantage can be taken of classroom pets.

Life Science

S1L1a. Identify the basic needs of a plant.
1. Air
2. Water
3. Light
4. Nutrients

S1L1c. Identify the parts of a plant—root, stem, leaf, and flower.

172 • Chapter 5   173

Georgia Science Performance Standards are identified for each chapter.

xiii

Every lesson in your book has two parts.

Part 1: Directed Inquiry

Science and You helps you think about the science facts.

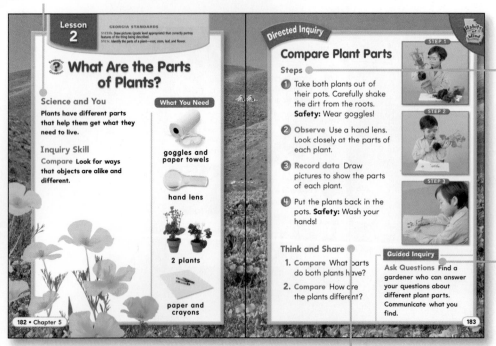

Steps to follow for the activity.

Guided Inquiry lets you do more on your own.

Georgia Science Standards appear throughout the lesson.

Think and Share lets you check what you have learned.

Part 2: Learn by Reading

Vocabulary lists the new science words you will learn. In the text, dark words with yellow around them are new words.

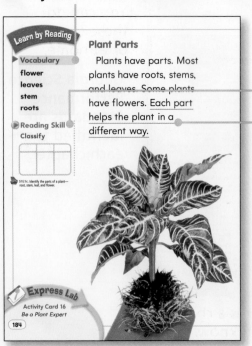

Reading Skill helps you understand the text.

Main Idea is underlined to show you what is important.

After you read, check what you have learned.

Lesson Wrap-Up

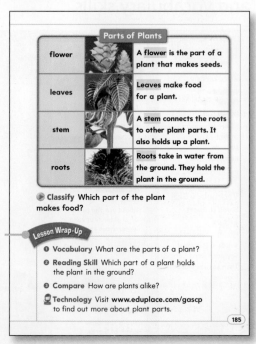

Focus On

Focus On lets you learn more about an important topic. Look for History of Science, Technology, Literature, Readers' Theater—and more.

Extreme Science

Extreme Science compares and contrasts interesting science informaion.

Links and Performance Task

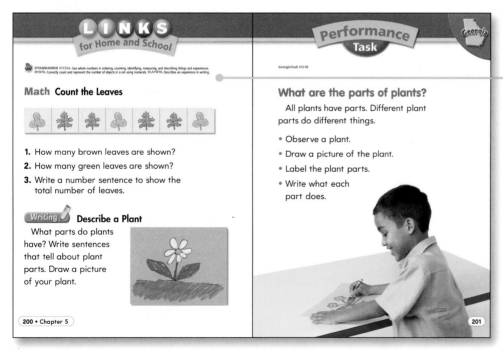

You can do these at school or at home.

Links connects science to other subject areas.

Performance Task is a chance to show what you know.

Review and Unit Practice

These reviews help you to know you are on track with learning Georgia science standards.

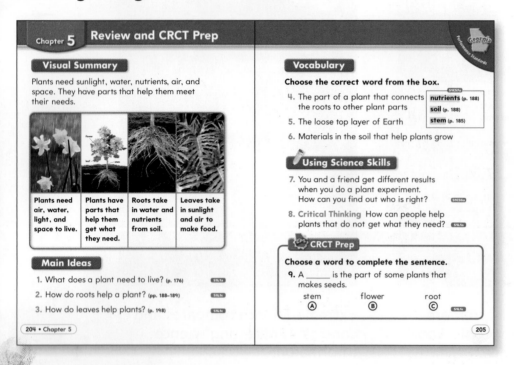

Chapter 5 Review and CRCT Prep

Visual Summary

Plants need sunlight, water, nutrients, air, and space. They have parts that help them meet their needs.

| Plants need air, water, light, and space to live. | Plants have parts that help them get what they need. | Roots take in water and nutrients from soil. | Leaves take in sunlight and air to make food. |

Main Ideas

1. What does a plant need to live? (p. 176)
2. How do roots help a plant? (pp. 188–189)
3. How do leaves help plants? (p. 198)

204 • Chapter 5

Vocabulary

Choose the correct word from the box.

4. The part of a plant that connects the roots to other plant parts
5. The loose top layer of Earth
6. Materials in the soil that help plants grow

nutrients (p. 188)
soil (p. 188)
stem (p. 185)

Using Science Skills

7. You and a friend get different results when you do a plant experiment. How can you find out who is right?
8. Critical Thinking How can people help plants that do not get what they need?

CRCT Prep

Choose a word to complete the sentence.

9. A _____ is the part of some plants that makes seeds.

   stem   flower   root
    Ⓐ   Ⓑ   Ⓒ

205

Unit Wrap-Up

C Wrap-Up

STANDARDS S1L1d. Contains and classes whose animals—reproduction, name, growth, basic needs.

You Can...

Discover More

What bird flaps its wings the fastest?

A hummingbird flaps its wings about 75 times every second! The wings move so fast that they make a humming sound. Hummingbirds are called nature's helicopters because of the way they move.

Go to **www.eduplace.com/gascp** to learn more about the parts of a hummingbird.

242 • Unit C

Learn more about science using the **Discover More!** question.

References

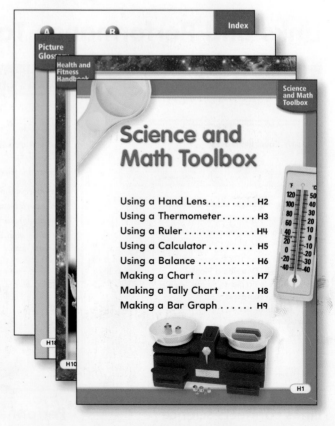

The back of your book includes sections you will refer to again and again.

S1CS3 Students will use tools and instruments for observing, measuring, and manipulating objects in scientific activities.

a. Use ordinary hand tools and instruments to construct, measure, and look at objects.

b. Make something that can actually be used to perform a task, using paper, cardboard, wood, plastic, metal, or existing objects.

c. Identify and practice accepted safety procedures in manipulating science materials and equipment.

S1CS4 Students will use the ideas of system, model, change, and scale in exploring scientific and technological matters.

a. Use a model—such as a toy or a picture—to describe a feature of the primary thing.

b. Describe changes in the size, weight, color, or movement of things, and note which of their other qualities remain the same during a specific change.

c. Compare very different sizes, weights, ages (baby/adult), and speeds (fast/slow) of both human made and natural things.

S1CS5 Students will communicate scientific ideas and activities clearly.

a. Describe and compare things in terms of number, shape, texture, size, weight, color, and motion.

b. Draw pictures (grade level appropriate) that correctly portray features of the thing being described.

c. Use simple pictographs and bar graphs to communicate data.

The Nature of Science

S1CS6 Students will be familiar with the character of scientific knowledge and how it is achieved.

Students will recognize that:

a. When a science investigation is done the way it was done before, we expect to get a similar result.

b. Science involves collecting data and testing hypotheses.

c. Scientists often repeat experiments multiple times, and subject their ideas to criticism by other scientists who may disagree with them and do further tests.

d. All different kinds of people can be and are scientists.

S1CS7 Students will understand important features of the process of scientific inquiry.

Students will apply the following to inquiry learning practices:

a. Scientists use a common language with precise definitions of terms to make it easier to communicate their observations to each other.

b. In doing science, it is often helpful to work as a team. All team members should reach individual conclusions and share their understandings with other members of the team in order to develop a consensus.

c. Tools such as thermometers, rulers, and balances often give more information about things than can be obtained by just observing things without help.

d. Much can be learned about plants and animals by observing them closely, but care must be taken to know the needs of living things and how to provide for them. Advantage can be taken of classroom pets.

Coverage of these standards occurs in Directed Inquiry, Guided Inquiry, and in other features.

Content Standards

Earth Science

S1E1 Students will observe, measure, and communicate weather data to see patterns in weather and climate.

a. Identify different types of weather and the characteristics of each type.

b. Investigate weather by observing, measuring with simple weather instruments (thermometer, wind vane, rain gauge), and recording weather data (temperature, precipitation, sky conditions, and weather events) in a periodic journal or on a calendar seasonally.

c. Correlate weather data (temperature, precipitation, sky conditions, and weather events) to seasonal changes.

Chapter 1: Weather and Seasons

S1E2 Students will observe and record changes in water as it relates to weather.

a. Recognize changes in water when it freezes (ice) and when it melts (water).

b. Identify forms of precipitation such as rain, snow, sleet, and hailstones as either solid (ice) or liquid (water).

c. Determine that the weight of water before freezing, after freezing, and after melting stays the same.

d. Determine that water in an open container disappears into the air over time, but water in a closed container does not.

Chapter 1: Weather and Seasons
Chapter 2: Water and Weather

Physical Science

S1P1 Students will investigate light and sound.

a. Recognize sources of light.

b. Explain how shadows are made.

c. Investigate how vibrations produce sound.

d. Differentiate between various sounds in terms of (pitch) high or low and (volume) loud or soft.

e. Identify emergency sounds and sounds that help us stay safe.

Chapter 3: Heat, Light, and Sound

S1P2 Students will demonstrate effects of magnets on other magnets and other objects.

a. Demonstrate how magnets attract and repel.

b. Identify common objects that are attracted to a magnet.

c. Identify objects and materials (air, water, wood, paper, your hand, etc.) that do not block magnetic force.

Chapter 4: Magnets

Life Science

S1L1 Students will investigate the characteristics and basic needs of plants and animals.

    a. Identify the basic needs of a plant.

        1. Air

        2. Water

        3. Light

        4. Nutrients

    b. Identify the basic needs of an animal.

        1. Air

        2. Water

        3. Food

        4. Shelter

    c. Identify the parts of a plant—root, stem, leaf, and flower.

    d. Compare and describe various animals—appearance, motion, growth, basic needs.

Chapter 5: Plants
Chapter 6: Animals

The Nature of Science

Science is an adventure. People all over the world do science. You can do science, too. You probably already do.

Start with Your Standards

The Nature of Science

S1CS6 Students will be familiar with the character of scientific knowledge and how it is achieved.

Students will recognize that:

   a. When a science investigation is done the way it was done before, we expect to get a similar result.

   b. Science involves collecting data and testing hypotheses.

   c. Scientists often repeat experiments multiple times, and subject their ideas to criticism by other scientists who may disagree with them and do further tests.

   d. All different kinds of people can be and are scientists.

S1CS7 Students will understand important features of the process of scientific inquiry.

Students will apply the following to inquiry learning practices:

   a. Scientists use a common language with precise definitions of terms to make it easier to communicate their observations to each other.

   b. In doing science, it is often helpful to work as a team. All team members should reach their own individual conclusions and share their understandings with other members of the team in order to develop a consensus.

   c. Tools such as thermometers, rulers, and balances often give more information about things than can be obtained by just observing things without help.

   d. Much can be learned about plants and animals by observing them closely, but care must be taken to know the needs of living things and how to provide for them. Advantage can be taken of classroom pets.

The Nature of Science

You Can...

Do What Scientists Do

Donna House planned this wetland and woods. Ms. House is a scientist. She studies plants and how native people use them. She protects plants that are in danger of dying out.

Scientists Investigate

Scientists ask questions. They answer them by observing and testing. Donna House gathers facts about plants. She reads about plants. She uses tools to measure plants. She talks to other scientists. She talks to elders in different tribes.

Donna House chose the wild plants around the National Museum of the American Indian in Washington, D.C.

Meet Donna House. She says you can learn a lot by taking walks outdoors with your elders.

Think Like a Scientist

Everyone can do science. To think like a scientist you have to:

- ▶ ask a lot of questions.

- ▶ work with others and listen to their ideas.

- ▶ try things over and over again.

- ▶ tell what really happens, not what you wanted to happen.

Do goldfish have eyelids? It looks like goldfish never close their eyes.

I read that goldfish do not have eyelids.

If the sunlight is too bright for their eyes, they swim to a shady spot.

Use Critical Thinking

Scientists use observations and other facts to answer their questions. A fact can be checked to make sure it is true. An opinion is what you think about the facts.

When you think, "That can't be true," you are thinking critically. Critical thinkers question what they hear.

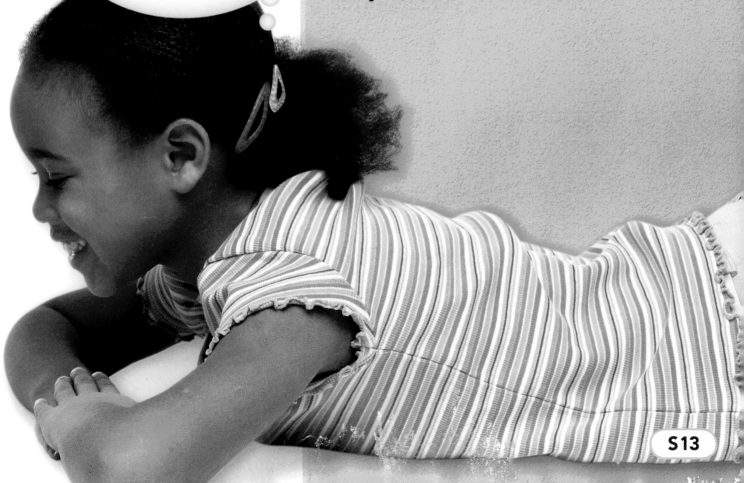

Science Inquiry

You can use **science inquiry** to learn about the world around you. Say you are playing with magnets.

Observe It seems like when I hold the magnets one way, they push apart. When I turn one magnet, they stick.

Ask a Question I wonder, are some parts of round magnets stronger than other parts?

Form an Idea I think some parts of round magnets are stronger than others.

Experiment I will need a round magnet and some paper clips. I will count how many paper clips the round magnet picks up. I will test different places on the magnet.

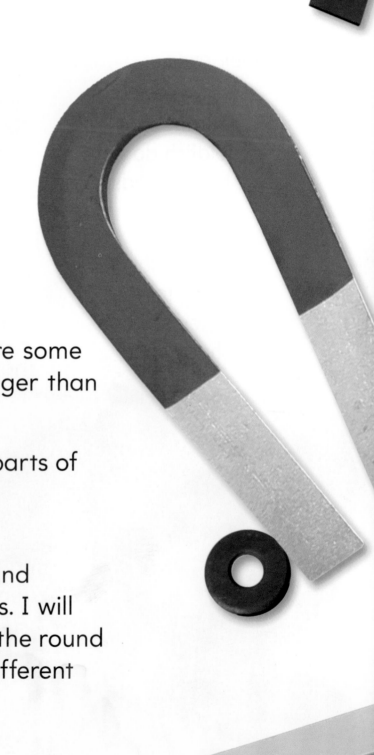

Conclusion I found that a round magnet picks up more paper clips on one side. So, my idea is supported. Round magnets do have parts that are stronger.

Communicate what you learn. You can use words or pictures. Tell others to try it themselves. You can expect them to get the same results.

Inquiry Process

Here is how some scientists answer questions and make new discoveries.

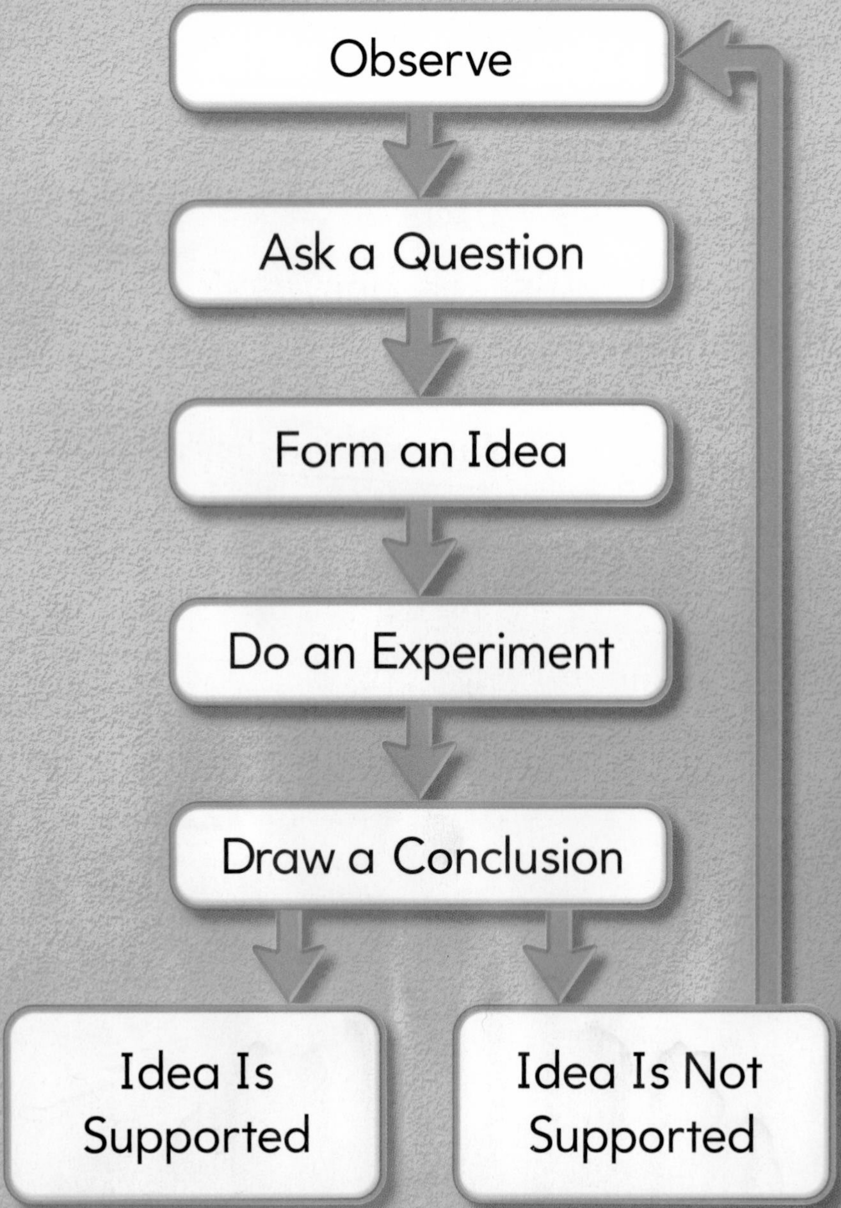

Observe

↓

Ask a Question

↓

Form an Idea

↓

Do an Experiment

↓

Draw a Conclusion

↓ ↓

Idea Is Supported

Idea Is Not Supported

GPS **STANDARDS S1CS6b.** Science involves collecting data and testing hypotheses.
S1CS6c. Scientists often repeat experiments multiple times, and subject their ideas to
criticism by other scientists who may disagree with them and do further tests.

Try It Yourself!

Experiment With a Diving Squid

Squeeze the bottle. The squid sinks.
Stop squeezing. The squid floats.

1 What questions do you have about the squid?

2 How would you find the answers?

3 Make a plan to test your idea. Tell what you think you will find out.

Be an Inventor

Neil Dermody had trouble finding his seat belt when he was eight years old. His mom asked him to invent a way to solve the problem.

First, Neil thought of putting light bulbs on the seat belt. He decided that the bulbs might break. Then he thought of things that glow in the dark.

Neil painted the buckle with paint that glowed in the dark. He sewed glow-in-the-dark fabric to the strap. It worked just fine.

Neil Dermody wins first prize for his invention.

"My mom always said, 'What problem are you having? How can you fix it?'"

What Is Technology?

The tools people make and use are **technology.** Paint that glows in the dark is technology. So is a hybrid car.

Scientists use technology. They use telescopes to study things that are far from Earth. They also use tools to measure things.

Technology can make life easier. Sometimes it causes problems too. Cars make it easy for people to travel. But a car's gas and oil can pollute the air.

A Better Idea

"I wish I had a better way to _____."
How would you fill in the blank?
Everyone can invent new things
and ideas. Even you!

An electric toothbrush
is fun to use. It also
cleans teeth better.

How to Be an Inventor

① **Find a problem.** It may be at school, at home, or in your neighborhood.

② **Think of a way to solve the problem.** List some ways to solve the problem. Decide which one will work best.

③ **Make a sample and try it out.** Your idea may need many materials or none at all. Try it out many times.

④ **Make your invention better.** Use what you learned to make changes.

⑤ **Share your invention.** Tell how your invention makes an activity easier or more fun. If it did not work well, tell why.

Make Decisions

Throwing Paper Away

How much paper does your class throw away? Most paper and other trash is buried in the ground. It takes up a lot of space.

Paper is made from mashed wood. Many trees are cut down to make paper. A lot of water is used. A lot of energy is used too.

Scrap Paper To Reuse

Deciding What to Do

How could your class throw away less paper?

Here's how to make your decision. You can use the same steps to help solve problems in your home or neighborhood.

Learn → Learn about the problem. Find the facts. You could talk to an expert or read a book.

List → List actions you could take. Add actions other people could take.

Decide → Decide which action is best for you, your school, or your neighborhood.

Share → Tell others what you decide.

Science Safety

Know the safety rules of your classroom and follow them. Follow the safety tips in your science book.

▶ **Wear safety goggles when your teacher tells you.**

▶ **Keep your work area clean. Tell your teacher about spills right away.**

▶ **Learn how to care for the plants and animals in your classroom.**

▶ **Wash your hands when you are done.**

Earth Science

Weather patterns can
be observed, measured,
and described.

Go Wind

by Lillian Moore

Go wind, blow
Push wind, swoosh.
    Shake things
    take things
    make things
            fly.

Ring things
swing things
fling things
        high.

Go wind, blow
Push things
wheee.
        No, wind, no.
        Not me —
        not *me.*

What Is Weather Like in Georgia?

Summer Weather?

**Hot and sticky!
How do you cool off?**

17° below zero!
January 27, 1940
was Georgia's **coldest**
day ever.

112°
July 24, 1953
was Georgia's **hottest**
day ever.

Floyd County

Atlanta

Louisville

GEORGIA

Winter Weather?

Cool.
Grab your jacket.
Most Georgia winters are mild.

**Brrr!
But Georgia can get
ice storms, too!**

Choose a word to complete the sentence.

1. Summer weather in Georgia is mostly

Ⓐ cold.

Ⓑ hot.

Ⓒ cool.

 S1E1a

Performance Task

Draw What to Wear

Draw pictures of what clothes to wear during different kinds of weather. Label your pictures.

GeorgiaTask S1E1H

Hands-On Project

GPS **STANDARDS S1CS3b.** Make something that can actually be used to perform a task, using paper, cardboard, wood, plastic, metal, or existing objects. **GeorgiaTask S1E1A**

Measure Weather

How can you find out about weather near school? Make a weather center to observe and measure weather.

What You Need

- frozen juice container
- paper
- poster board
- rulers
- tape
- thermometer
- wooden stick

Step 1: Plan

- Make a rain gauge. Place it outdoors to collect rain.

- Make a wind vane. Place it outdoors.

- Place the thermometer outdoors.

Step 2: Do It

- **Measure** the weather each day for two weeks. Check each tool. Write or draw how the sky looks.

- Record your data in a chart.

Step 3: Share

- Talk about how the weather changed. Put your weather data in a book.

Week 1

	Monday	Tuesday	Wednesday
How the sky looks	Clouds	sunny	clouds
Rain	yes	no	yes
Wind	yes	no	no
Temperature	57°F	63°F	61°F

Chapter 1

Weather and Seasons

Lesson Preview

LESSON 1
Weather changes every day. How is today's weather different from yesterday's weather?

LESSON 2

You can use tools to find out about weather. What does a thermometer tell you?

LESSON 3
You see gray clouds low in the sky. How might the weather change?

LESSON 4

Many plants bloom in spring. Why does this happen?

LESSON 5
People find different ways to cool off in summer. Why do they do that?

Vocabulary Preview

Vocabulary

Vocabulary Skill

Use Words

thermometer

Use a thermometer to find out how hot the air is. Find other words in the sentence that tell what a thermometer is.

weather
Weather is what the air outside is like.

thermometer
A thermometer is a tool that measures temperature.

season
A season is a time of year that has its own kind of weather.

cloud

Many drops of water together form a cloud.

Start with Your Standards

Habits of Mind

S1CS3b. Make something that can actually be used to perform a task, using paper, cardboard, wood, plastic, metal, or existing objects.

S1CS4a. Use a model—such as a toy or a picture—to describe a feature of the primary thing.

The Nature of Science

S1CS6b. Science involves collecting data and testing hypotheses.

Earth Science

S1E1a. Identify different types of weather and the characteristics of each type.

S1E1b. Investigate weather by observing, measuring with simple weather instruments (thermometer, wind vane, rain gauge), and recording weather data (temperature, precipitation, sky conditions, and weather events) in a periodic journal or on a calendar seasonally.

S1E1c. Correlate weather data (temperature, precipitation, sky conditions, and weather events) to seasonal changes.

S1E2d. Determine that water in an open container disappears into the air over time, but water in a closed container does not.

Lesson 1

GEORGIA STANDARDS

S1CS4a. Use a model—such as a toy or a picture—to describe a feature of the primary thing.
S1E1a. Identify different types of weather and the characteristics of each type.

Essential Question

What Is Weather?

Science and You

Observing the weather can help you decide to play inside or outside.

Inquiry Skill

Record Data You can use pictures to show what you observe.

What You Need

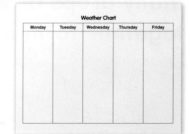

weather chart

weather pictures

scissors

glue

Habits of Mind

Record Weather

Steps

1. **Observe** Look outside to see the weather today.

STEP 1

2. Cut out pictures that show the weather today. **Safety:** Scissors are sharp!

STEP 2

3. **Record Data** Glue the pictures in your weather chart.

4. Repeat each day for one week.

STEP 3

Think and Share

1. What does your chart tell you about the weather?

2. Why might you record two pictures for the same day?

Guided Inquiry

Work Together Record the weather for two more weeks. Talk with others. Were their data the same or different? Tell why.

▶ **Vocabulary**

weather

◉ **Reading Skill**
**Main Idea
and Details**

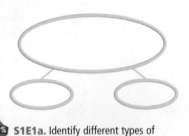

GPS **S1E1a.** Identify different types of
weather and the characteristics of
each type.

Kinds of Weather

Weather is what the air outside is like. There are many kinds of weather. Weather may be warm or cool. It may be rainy or sunny. It may be cloudy or windy.

How do you know it is warm and sunny here?

You can use your senses to observe the weather. You can see clouds. You can hear rain. You can feel warm or cool air. You can see wind move things.

▶ **Main Idea** What are some kinds of weather?

rainy ▼

▲ windy and cloudy

Ways Weather Changes

Monday	cloudy	
Tuesday	rainy	
Wednesday	sunny	

Weather Changes

Weather changes when the air changes. Weather can change from day to day. One day the weather can be sunny and warm. The next day it can be cloudy and cool. Then clouds may bring rain.

▶ **Main Idea** How might weather change from day to day?

Lesson Wrap-Up

❶ **Vocabulary** Tell something that you know about **weather**.

❷ **Reading Skill** How can you use your senses to observe weather?

❸ **Record Data** Tell one way to record data.

Technology Visit **www.eduplace.com/gascp** to find out more about weather.

GPS GEORGIA STANDARDS

S1CS3b. Make something that can actually be used to perform a task, using paper, cardboard, wood, plastic, metal, or existing objects.

S1E1b. Investigate weather by observing, measuring with simple weather instruments (thermometer, wind vane, rain gauge), and recording weather data (temperature, precipitation, sky conditions, and weather events) in a periodic journal or on a calendar seasonally.

Essential Question: How Can You Measure Weather?

Science and You

Reading a thermometer helps you know when you might need a jacket.

Inquiry Skill

Measure Use a tool to find how much or how many.

What You Need

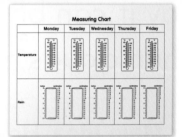

measuring chart

thermometer

ruler

rain collector

Measure Weather

Steps

① Take the thermometer and the rain collector outside.

STEP 1

② **Record Data** Go outside again later. Read the thermometer. Record the temperature.

STEP 2

③ **Measure** Use a ruler to measure any rain. Record what you measure. Empty the rain collector.

④ Do these steps for five days.

STEP 3

Think and Share

1. How did tools help you learn about weather?

2. How did the weather change during the five days?

Guided Inquiry

Be an Inventor Invent a tool to show if wind is blowing. Try your tool. Explain how your tool works.

Habits of Mind

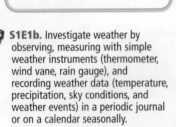

Vocabulary

thermometer
temperature

▶ **Reading Skill**
Draw Conclusions

S1E1b. Investigate weather by observing, measuring with simple weather instruments (thermometer, wind vane, rain gauge), and recording weather data (temperature, precipitation, sky conditions, and weather events) in a periodic journal or on a calendar seasonally.

A Tool for Temperature

One way to tell about weather is to use tools. A **thermometer** is a tool that measures temperature. **Temperature** is how warm or cool something is.

What do these thermometers tell about the weather?

Knowing the temperature helps you know what to wear. In cold temperature, you wear clothes that keep you warm. When it is hot, you wear clothes that keep you cool.

▶ **Draw Conclusions** If you need a coat, what can you tell about the temperature?

Express Lab

Activity Card 2
Compare Temperatures

Tools for Wind and Rain

You can use tools to measure wind and rain. A windsock and a wind vane show which way the wind blows. A windsock also shows how hard the wind blows. A rain gauge measures how much rain falls.

▶ **Draw Conclusions** If a rain gauge is full, what can you tell about the weather?

▼ **windsock**

wind vane ▼

rain gauge ▶

Lesson Wrap-Up

❶ Vocabulary What is **temperature**?

❷ Reading Skill If a windsock is hanging down, what can you tell about the wind?

❸ Measure How can you describe weather?

Technology Visit **www.eduplace.com/gascp** to find out more about weather tools.

25

Read the page from the story. Then read the poem. Compare how the writers observe rain.

Rain
by Manya Stojic

A raindrop splashed.
"The rain is here!"
said the rhino.

"Porcupine smelled it.
The zebras saw it.
The baboons heard it.
And I felt it.
I must tell the lion."

STANDARDS S1E1a. Identify different types of weather and the characteristics of each type.

READING LINK

City Rain

by Rachel Field

Rain in the city!
  I love to see it fall
Slantwise where the
buildings crowd
  Red brick and all,
Streets of shiny wetness
  Where the taxis go,
With people and umbrellas all
  Bobbing to and fro.

Sharing Ideas

1. **Write About It** How do the animals and the poet know it is raining?

2. **Talk About It** What is one thing in the story that real animals cannot do?

27

Lesson 3

GEORGIA STANDARDS

S1CS2a. Use whole numbers in ordering, counting, identifying, measuring, and describing things and experiences.
S1E2d. Determine that water in an open container disappears into the air over time, but water in a closed container does not.

What Are Clouds and Rain?

Science and You

If you see dark clouds in the sky, you know it might rain.

Inquiry Skill

Compare Look for ways that objects are alike and different.

What You Need

2 cups

water

tape

plastic wrap

grease pencil

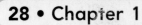

Water Changes

Steps

STEP 1

1️⃣ **Measure** Put the same amount of water into each cup. Cover one cup.

2️⃣ Mark the water level on each cup.

STEP 2

3️⃣ **Predict** Put the cups in a sunny place. Tell how the water might change.

4️⃣ **Observe** Look at the cups every day for a week. Record what you see.

STEP 3

Think and Share

1. **Compare** How did the water change in each cup?

2. **Infer** Why do you think the water changed?

Guided Inquiry

Ask Questions What else can you do to make water change? Finish the question. What would happen to the water if I _____?

▶ **Vocabulary**

water cycle
cloud

▶ **Reading Skill**
Cause and Effect

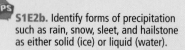

S1E2b. Identify forms of precipitation such as rain, snow, sleet, and hailstone as either solid (ice) or liquid (water).

Water Cycle

Water moves from place to place. Sometimes it seems to disappear. Water moving from Earth to the sky and back again is called the **water cycle**.

▶ **Cause and Effect**
What causes water to go into the air?

1 Heat from the Sun warms water. Some warm water goes into the air. You cannot see this water.

2 Water in the air cools.
Tiny drops of water form.
Many drops of water
together form a **cloud**.

3 Water drops in the
clouds get bigger.
Then they fall back to
Earth as rain or sleet.

Express Lab

Activity Card 3
Compare Clouds

Kinds of Clouds

There are many kinds of clouds. They have different shapes and colors. Looking at clouds gives you clues about changing weather.

▶ **Cause and Effect** What can clouds tell you about changing weather?

Cirrus clouds are thin and feathery. They mean it may rain in a day or two.

Cumulus clouds are puffy and white. They can turn gray and bring rain.

Stratus clouds are low and gray. They may bring rain or snow.

Lesson Wrap-Up

❶ **Vocabulary** What is the **water cycle**?

❷ **Reading Skill** What causes rain to fall?

❸ **Compare** Draw two kinds of clouds. Tell how they are alike and different.

Technology Visit **www.eduplace.com/gascp** to find out more about clouds.

GPS GEORGIA STANDARDS

S1CS4b. Describe changes in the size, weight, color, or movement of things, and note which of their other qualities remain the same during a specific change.

S1E1c. Correlate weather data (temperature, precipitation, sky conditions, and weather events) to seasonal changes.

Essential Question

What Is Weather Like In Spring and Summer?

Science and You

Spring is a time when you may see flowers bloom.

Inquiry Skill

Communicate Tell other people what you know by drawing, speaking, or writing.

What You Need

2 cups

paper towels

seeds

water

Habits of Mind

Grow Plants

Steps

STEP 1

1. Spray water on the paper towels. Fill each cup with paper towels.

2. Add seeds to each cup.

STEP 2

3. **Predict** Put the **winter** cup in a cold place. Put the **spring** cup in a warm place. Tell what you think will happen.

4. **Communicate** Look at the seeds after five days. Talk about how they have changed.

STEP 3

Think and Share

1. What helped the seeds grow?

2. **Infer** What happens to seeds in cold weather?

Guided Inquiry

Experiment Put the sprouted seeds in soil. Make a plan for caring for the plants. Follow your plan. Observe the plants for one month.

Vocabulary

season

spring

summer

▶ **Reading Skill**
Compare and
Contrast

S1E1c. Correlate weather data (temperature, precipitation, sky conditions, and weather events) to seasonal changes.

Spring

A **season** is a time of year that has its own kind of weather. **Spring** is the season that follows winter. There are more hours of daylight in spring than in winter.

In spring, the weather begins to get warmer. Warmer weather and spring rain help plants grow.

Spring plants begin to grow.

The warm weather and new plants make it easy for animals to find food. Animals that slept all winter are now awake. Birds that flew to other places in winter have come back. Many baby animals are born in spring.

goose with gosling

▶ **Compare and Contrast** How is spring different from winter?

Luna Moth in Spring

1 A caterpillar eats a leaf.

2 A caterpillar spins a cocoon.

3 A caterpillar changes to a moth.

Summer

Summer is the season that follows spring. <u>Summer is the warmest season of the year.</u> It has the most hours of daylight.

In summer, people try to find ways to stay cool. They wear clothing that keeps them cool. They might go swimming to cool off.

How is this girl keeping cool?

Express Lab

Activity Card 4
Show Summer Weather

Summer is the season for plants and animals to grow. Fruits form on trees and bushes. Young animals learn to find their own food.

peach tree

 **Compare and Contrast**
How are spring and summer different?

▲ **Growing plants are food for the lamb.**

Lesson Wrap-Up

❶ **Vocabulary** What is a **season**?

❷ **Reading Skill** How are spring and summer alike?

❸ **Communicate** Write a story or draw a picture. Tell what happens to plants or animals in spring or summer.

Technology Visit **www.eduplace.com/gascp** to find out more about seasons.

EXTREME Science

So Hot! So Cold!

Freezing cold? Burning Hot? No problem! These animals do just fine living in some of the coldest winters and hottest summers on Earth.

◀ **Ouch! This lizard lives in a hot desert. Its scaly skin protects it from the desert heat.**

▼ **Brrrr! Penguins live where the weather is icy cold. Layers of fat and thick feathers protect penguins from the cold.**

Lesson 5

GEORGIA STANDARDS

S1CS5b. Draw pictures (grade level appropriate) that correctly portray features of the thing being described.
S1E1c. Correlate weather data (temperature, precipitation, sky conditions, and weather events) to seasonal changes.

Essential Question

What Is Weather Like in Fall and Winter?

Science and You

When you know about the seasons, you know what kind of weather is coming next.

Inquiry Skill

Classify Group objects that are alike in some way.

What You Need

spinner

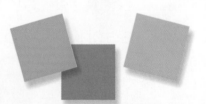

paper squares

crayons

paper

Habits of Mind

What to Wear

Steps

1 Take turns spinning the spinner.

STEP 1

2 **Communicate** Name a clothing item you might wear in that season. Draw the item you name.

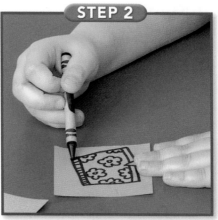
STEP 2

3 **Classify** Sort the clothing pictures by season. Label each group.

STEP 3

winter   spring

summer   fall

Think and Share

1. **Compare** How are all the summer clothes you drew alike?

2. What clothes keep you warm in cool weather?

Guided Inquiry

Solve a Problem Suppose your cousins are coming to visit you in winter. What kind of clothes would you tell them to bring?

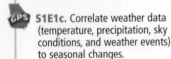

Learn by Reading

Vocabulary

fall

winter

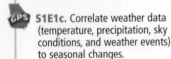

▶ **Reading Skill**

Sequence

```
┌─────────────────┐
│                 │
└─────────────────┘
        ↓
┌─────────────────┐
│                 │
└─────────────────┘
        ↓
┌─────────────────┐
│                 │
└─────────────────┘
```

GPS **S1E1c.** Correlate weather data (temperature, precipitation, sky conditions, and weather events) to seasonal changes.

Fall

Fall is the season that follows summer. There are fewer hours of daylight in fall than in summer.

In fall, the weather gets cooler. People wear warmer clothes. Some leaves turn color and fall to the ground. Many fruits and vegetables are ripe.

Geese fly to warm places in fall.

In fall, animals get ready for cold weather. Some animals grow thicker fur to keep warm. Many animals store food for winter. Other animals move to places where there is more food. They will return in spring.

▶ **Sequence** What season comes before winter?

A squirrel stores food for winter.

Winter

Winter is the season that follows fall. Winter has the fewest hours of daylight. It is the coldest season of the year. In some places, snow falls and water freezes. In other places, winter weather is warmer.

winter where weather is warm ▶

◀ winter where weather is cold

Why is it hard for animals to find food here?

Sometimes it is hard for animals to find food in winter. Some plants die. Many trees lose their leaves. Many animals eat food that they gathered in fall. Some animals sleep all winter.

▶ **Sequence** What season follows winter?

Express Lab

Activity Card 5
Show Winter Weather

47

The Pattern of Seasons

The seasons change in the same order every year. Living things change with the seasons.

❶ **Vocabulary** What is **winter**?

❷ **Reading Skill** What season comes before fall?

❸ **Classify** Name three signs of fall.

🖥 **Technology** Visit **www.eduplace.com/gascp** to find out more about seasons.

GPS **STANDARDS** S1CS6d. All different kinds of people can be and are scientists.

Betty Davis

Betty Davis knows about weather. She and her team use tools to predict the weather. Then she reports the weather on television.

Betty is good at what she does. She worked hard in school. She wants you to work hard, too!

Betty Davis predicts the weather.

DOPPLER RADAR

RAIN · MIX · SNOW · Past 24 Hours

ER RADAR

HEAVY

Great Falls

Billings

49

LINKS
for Home and School

 STANDARDS **S1CS5c.** Use simple pictographs and bar graphs to communicate data. **M1D1a.** Interpret tally marks, picture graphs, and bar graphs. **ELA1W1b.** Describes an experience in writing.

Math Read a Bar Graph

Ms. Lane's class made a bar graph to show the weather for eight days.

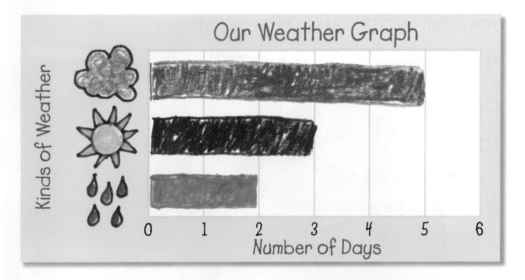

1. How many days were sunny?

2. How many more days were cloudy than rainy?

Writing Describe Weather

Tell about winter where you live. Draw a picture of yourself in winter.

Winter is warm where I live.

Georgia

How do weather patterns change?

Weather changes from season to season. Make a book to show the weather for each season.

- Tell about temperature.

- Tell how much rain falls during each season.

- Add pictures to your book.

Visual Summary

Weather changes from day to day and from season to season.

Weather Changes

day to day	sunny	rainy	cloudy	windy
season to season	winter	spring	summer	fall

Main Ideas

1. What are some kinds of weather? (p. 16)   `S1E1a`

2. What can you tell by looking at clouds? (p. 32)   `S1E1a`

3. What is a season? (p. 36)   `S1E1c`

4. How does weather change from summer to fall? (p. 44)   `S1E1c`

Vocabulary

Choose the correct word from the box.

S1CS7a

cloud (p. 31)

summer (p. 38)

thermometer (p. 22)

winter (p. 46)

5. A tool that measures temperature

6. Many drops of water together

7. The season that follows fall

8. The season that follows spring

Using Science Skills

9. **Classify** List three things that tell you about spring. **S1E1c**

10. **Critical Thinking** How do you know it is windy if you cannot see the wind? **S1E1a**

GPS CRCT Prep

Choose a word to complete the sentence.

11. Water moving from Earth to the sky and back again is the

Ⓐ spring. Ⓑ water cycle. Ⓒ weather.

S1E2b

Chapter 2

Water and Weather

Lesson Preview

LESSON 1

Water falls from the sky in warm and cold weather. How does water change with the temperature?

LESSON 2

Why does it snow in some places and not others?

Vocabulary

rain p. 60

freeze p. 61

melt p. 62

snow p. 68

sleet p. 69

hail p. 70

Picture Glossary p. H18

Vocabulary Skill

Classify Words

freeze

To freeze is to change from a liquid to a solid. When water freezes, it changes to ice.

Find all the words that name frozen water. Say each word.

sleet
Sleet is water that falls as frozen or partly frozen raindrops.

hail

Hail is round ice and hard snow that falls during thunderstorms.

rain

Rain is water that falls in drops from clouds.

snow

Snow is ice that falls from clouds.

Georgia

Performance Standards

Start with Your Standards

Habits of Mind

S1CS2d. Make quantitative estimates of familiar lengths, weights, and time intervals, and check them by measuring.

S1CS3a. Use ordinary hand tools and instruments to construct, measure, and look at objects.

S1CS5a. Describe and compare things in terms of number, shape, texture, size, weight, color, and motion.

Earth Science

S1E2a. Recognize changes in water when it freezes (ice) and when it melts (water).

S1E2b. Identify forms of precipitation such as rain, snow, sleet, and hailstones as either solid (ice) or liquid (water).

S1E2c. Determine that the weight of water before freezing, after freezing, and after melting stays the same.

GPS GEORGIA STANDARDS

S1CS3a. Use ordinary hand tools and instruments to construct, measure, and look at objects.
S1E2c. Determine that the weight of water before freezing, after freezing, and after melting stays the same.

? How Does Water Change?

Essential Question

Science and You

You can read a thermometer to find the temperature. If it is very cold it may snow. If it is warm it may rain.

Inquiry Skill

Measure Use a tool to find out how much or how many.

What You Need

bag of water

balance and gram cubes

Compare Water Chart			
	Water	Frozen Water	Melted Water
What does it look like?			
How does it feel?			
How many cubes did you use?			

Compare Water Chart

Compare Water

Steps

1 **Measure** Use a pan balance and cubes to measure the bag of water.

2 **Record Data** Write the number of cubes used.

3 **Measure** Freeze the bag overnight. Repeat steps 1 and 2 with the bag of ice.

4 Let the bag of ice melt in the pan. Repeat steps 1 and 2.

STEP 1

STEP 3

STEP 4

Think and Share

1. **Use Numbers** Did the number of cubes change?

2. **Compare** How does water change? How does water stay the same?

Guided Inquiry

Predict What will happen if you use another liquid and its frozen solid? Investigate with different kinds of liquid, such as apple juice.

Vocabulary

rain

freeze

melt

Reading Skill

Compare and Contrast

GPS **S1E2a.** Recognize changes in water when it freezes (ice) and when it melts (water).

Wet Weather

Water is part of weather. Water that falls in drops from clouds is **rain**. Rain is a liquid. Liquids take the shape of the container they are in. Rain is wet and clear.

Rain is water.

water

Water Freezes

Water changes when it gets very cold. If the temperature is 32°F, water will freeze into ice. To **freeze** is to change from a liquid to a solid. A solid keeps its shape. Ice is cold and hard.

▶ **Compare** What is the same about an ice cube and ice on a pond?

ice

Ice is solid water.

Express Lab

Activity Card 6
Measure Rainfall

Ice Melts

Ice changes when the temperature is warm. When it is warm ice melts. To **melt** is to change from a solid to a liquid. Melting ice changes back into water.

Why is the ice melting?

When the weather changes, water changes, too. Cold weather can change water into ice. Warm weather can change ice into a liquid.

Lesson Wrap-Up

❶ **Vocabulary** What is **rain**?

❷ **Reading Skill** What is different about water and ice? What is the same?

❸ **Measure** Which tool helps you measure how heavy something is?

Technology Visit **www.eduplace.com/gascp** to find out more about water and weather.

EXTREME science

 STANDARDS **S1E2b.** Identify forms of precipitation such as rain, snow, sleet, and hailstone as either solid (ice) or liquid (water).

FLASH FLOOD!

Sometimes it does not just rain. It pours! Strong thunderstorms can drop one inch of rain an hour! The rain comes down so fast, it has nowhere to go. Streets fill with water. Rivers overflow. In a "flash," you have a flood!

On one June day of 1999, thunderstorms dumped over ten inches of rain on Savannah, Georgia. This man had to use a surfboard to paddle home!

GEORGIA STANDARDS

S1CS5a. Describe and compare things in terms of number, shape, texture, size, weight, color, and motion.
S1E2b. Identify forms of precipitation such as rain, snow, sleet, and hailstones as either solid (ice) or liquid (water).

Essential Question

How Does Temperature Change Water?

Science and You

When it is cold you might get a snowy day.

Inquiry Skill

Observe You can use your senses to find out about something.

What You Need

can

ice

salt

chart

Observe Frost

Steps

1. **Communicate** Feel the inside and the outside of the can. Write down how it feels.

STEP 1

2. Put ice in the can. Add salt. Stir the salt in the can. Observe the inside and outside of the can.

STEP 2

3. **Compare** Wait 15 minutes. Feel the inside and the outside of the can again. Write down how it feels.

STEP 3

Think and Share

1. Where did you feel and see frost?

2. **Infer** What happened inside the can?

Guided Inquiry

Measure How cold is the air inside the can? Use a thermometer to find out.

▶ **Vocabulary**

snow

sleet

hail

▶ **Reading Skill**
Classify

S1E2b. Identify forms of precipitation such as rain, snow, sleet, and hailstones as either solid (ice) or liquid (water).

snowflake

Ice in Cold Weather

When air in clouds is very cold, water in clouds will freeze. Different kinds of ice fall from clouds. **Snow** is ice that falls from clouds. Falling snow is white and soft.

Sleet can be messy.

sleet

Another kind of ice that falls from clouds is sleet. **Sleet** is frozen or partly frozen raindrops. It is a mixture of rain and snow. Sleet is wet and slushy.

▶ **Classify** Is snow a solid or a liquid?

Ice in Warm Weather

Ice can fall from clouds when the weather is warm. **Hail** is round ice and hard snow. Hail falls during thunderstorms. Hail can be small or large.

Hail can be as small as a pebble or as large as a baseball.

Express Lab

Activity Card 7
Observe Ice

These storm clouds can bring hail.

High in the clouds air can become very cold. Water in clouds turns to ice. It falls as hail.

▶ **Classify** Is hail a solid or a liquid?

Lesson Wrap-Up

❶ **Vocabulary** What is **sleet**?

❷ **Reading Skill** How is sleet liquid and solid?

❸ **Observe** Describe what frost feels like and looks like.

💻 **Technology** Visit **www.eduplace.com/gascp** to find out more about frozen water.

The Snowflake Man

Wilson Bentley loved snow. He thought snowflakes were very pretty. He tried to draw pictures. He could not do it. The snowflakes melted.

Wilson Bentley photographing snowflakes

STANDARDS S1E2a. Recognize changes in water when it freezes (ice) and when it melts (water).

READING LINK

So Bentley used a special camera. It had a special lens. He caught snowflakes on black velvet. Then he took a picture. He had to be fast. He was the first person to take a close-up picture of a snowflake. Compare these three pictures of Bentley's snowflakes.

Sharing Ideas

1. **Talk About It** Tell why you think Wilson Bentley was called "The Snowflake Man."

2. **Write About It** Look closely at the snowflakes. Write about what you observe.

LINKS
for Home and School

STANDARDS S1CS2a. Use whole numbers in ordering, counting, identifying, measuring, and describing things and experiences. **M1D1.** Students will create sample tables and graphs and interpret them.

Math Recording Rainfall

Read the chart to find out how much rain fell in Atlanta, Georgia.

Rain in Atlanta			
January	April	July	October
5 inches	4 inches	5 inches	3 inches

1. How many inches of rain fell in April?

2. Which two months had the same inches of rainfall?

 **Write a Poem**

Reading down, the first letter of each line spells a word. Reading across, each line in the poem describes the word. Write a poem like this using a weather word.

Wet
Everywhere
Air
Thunderstorm
Hail
Enjoy playing in snow
Rain

Performance Task

STANDARDS S1CS2d. Make quantitative estimates of familiar lengths, weights, and time intervals, and check them by measuring. **GeorgiaTask S1E2D**

Measure a Puddle

You can see puddles after it rains. How long does it take for a puddle to dry?

- Use chalk to trace the outline of a puddle.

- Estimate how wide the puddle is. Then use a ruler to measure it.

- Check the puddle every 2 hours. Draw how the puddle changes.

Visual Summary

Water can fall from clouds as a solid or a liquid.

Rain	Snow	Sleet	Hail
liquid	solid	solid and partly solid	solid

Main Ideas

1. Tell what happens when liquid water freezes. (p. 61)   **S1E2a**

2. What happens to ice to make it melt? (p. 62)   **S1E2a**

3. Compare snow and sleet. (pp. 68–69)   **S1E2b**

4. When does hail fall to the ground? (p. 70)   **S1E2b**

Vocabulary

Choose the correct word from the box.

S1CS7a
freeze (p. 61)
melt (p. 62)
snow (p. 68)
sleet (p. 69)

5. water that falls as frozen or partly frozen raindrops

6. to change from a solid to a liquid

7. ice that falls from clouds

8. to change from a liquid to a solid

Using Science Skills

9. **Compare** How are rain and snow different? How are they the same?   S1E2b

10. **Critical Thinking** The sky is cloudy. How do you know if it will rain or snow?   S1E2b

GPS CRCT Prep

Choose a word to complete the sentence.

11. The temperature is very, very cold. Water is falling from the sky. It falls as _____

Ⓐ snow.   Ⓑ rain.   Ⓒ hail.   S1E2b

Test Practice

Choose the correct answer.

1. What does this tool measure?

rain	wind	temperature
Ⓐ	Ⓑ	Ⓒ

S1E1b

2. When water freezes it is a _____

liquid.	solid.	gas.
Ⓐ	Ⓑ	Ⓒ

S1E2a

3. Which thermometer shows the temperature in a cold season?

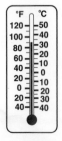  

Ⓐ	Ⓑ	Ⓒ

S1E1c

4. Which is a kind of weather?

rainy	the Sun	temperature
Ⓐ	Ⓑ	Ⓒ

S1E1a

5. Read the chart. Which day had snow?

Weather Chart			
Day	**Temperature**	**Wet or Dry?**	**Sunny or Cloudy?**
Thursday	warm	wet	partly sunny
Friday	very cold	wet	cloudy
Saturday	very cold	dry	sunny

Thursday
(A)

Friday
(B)

Saturday
(C)

S1E1c

GPS Checking Main Ideas

Write the correct answer.

6. Tell how weather changes from season to season.

S1E1c

7. How might this lake change if the temperature gets very cold?

S1E2a

Discover More

Why doesn't it snow everywhere in winter?

Because of Earth's shape and tilt, the Sun is high in the sky in places closer to the middle of Earth every day. These places get more light and heat from the Sun all year. During winter it is usually too warm to snow in these places.

Winter in California

Winter in Georgia

 Go to **www.eduplace.com/gascp** to see why it snows in some places during winter.

GEORGIA SCIENCE

UNIT
B

Physical Science

Cricket Connection

Visit www.eduplace.com/gascp
to check out *Click, Ask,* and
Odyssey magazine articles
and activities.

UNIT B

Physical Science

Independent Reading

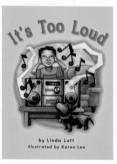

It's Too
Loud

Shadows

Night Lights

Georgia **Fun Facts**

A violin bow is
made of horsehair.
When it is drawn across
the strings, they vibrate.

Physical Science

Light and sound can be observed and measured. The effects of magnets can also be observed.

Magnets

Magnets push and pull;
They attract and repel.
They attract objects made with iron,
And they do it oh so well.

But my coat and water bottle
Are things magnets don't attract.
There's no push, there's no pull,
And that's a fact.

 from Science Songs, track 25

Science in Georgia

GPS STANDARDS S1P1d. Differentiate between various sounds in terms of (pitch) high or low and (volume) loud or soft.

How Are Sounds Different?

The farm may seem quiet. Listen closely. What sounds do you hear?

rooster

pig

COW

Science in Georgia

 STANDARDS S1P1d. Differentiate between various sounds in terms of (pitch) high or low and (volume) loud or soft. **S1P1e.** Identify emergency sounds and sounds that help us stay safe.

City Sounds

Cities are full of loud sounds. Horns are honking. Motors are running. Listen closely. What other sounds do you hear?

music

noise

Choose the best answer.

1. How are country sounds different from city sounds?

 They are softer.

Ⓑ They are louder.

Ⓒ They are the same.

S1P1d

Performance Task

Compare Sounds

Work with a partner. Use a tape recorder to tape sounds in your school. Listen to your tape. List the sounds that you hear. Sort the sounds: loud, soft, high, low.

GeorgiaTask S1P1B

GPS **STANDARDS S1CS3b.** Make something that can actually be used to perform a task, using paper, cardboard, wood, plastic, metal, or existing objects. **S1P1c.** Investigate how vibrations produce sound.

Make Instruments

How can you make music with sounds?
Make instruments to find out.

What You Need

- construction paper
- dried beans
- goggles
- paper towel tubes
- rubber bands
- scissors
- shoe box
- straws
- tape

Step 1: Plan

- Form a band with some classmates. Each band member can make an instrument.

Step 2: Do It

- Make a shaker. Use dried beans, paper, and a tube.

- Make a string instrument. Wrap a few rubber bands around a shoebox. **Safety!** Wear goggles.

- Make a wind instrument. Cut straws in different lengths. Tape them together.

- Make some music together!

Step 3: Share

- What kinds of sounds did each instrument make?

Chapter 3

Heat, Light, and Sound

Lesson Preview

LESSON 1

Heat from a fire keeps you warm. What else do you use heat for?

LESSON 2

Light from a lamp helps you to read. What else gives off light?

LESSON 3

Listen to the drumbeat. What sounds do you hear every day?

LESSON 4

A lion makes a loud sound. How are the sounds of a lion and a kitten different?

Vocabulary Preview

Vocabulary

Vocabulary Skill

Find All the Meanings

pitch

A word can have more than one meaning. You may know that the word **pitch** means to throw a ball. The word **pitch** also tells how high or low a sound is.

light
You can see light.

heat
Makes things warm.

sound
You can hear sound.

volume
Volume is how loud or
soft a sound is.

Georgia
Performance Standards

Start with Your Standards

Habits of Mind

S1CS3a. Use ordinary hand tools and
instruments to construct, measure, and
look at objects.

S1CS3c. Identify and practice accepted safety
procedures in manipulating science
materials and equipment.

The Nature of Science

S1CS6b. Science involves collecting data and
testing hypotheses.

Physical Science

S1P1a. Recognize sources of light.

S1P1b. Explain how shadows are made.

S1P1c. Investigate how vibrations produce
sound.

S1P1d. Differentiate between various sounds
in terms of (pitch) high or low and
(volume) loud or soft.

S1P1e. Identify emergency sounds and sounds
that help us stay safe.

GEORGIA STANDARDS

S1CS3a. Use ordinary hand tools and instruments to construct, measure, and look at objects.

S1P1a. Recognize sources of light.

Where Does Heat Come From?

Essential Question

Science and You

Heat from the Sun can make you hot and thirsty.

Inquiry Skill

Measure You can use a tool to find out how much or how many.

What You Need

3 jars

water and sand

3 thermometers

heat chart

Habits of Mind

Measure Heat

Steps

1. Fill one jar with water. Fill another jar with sand. Leave one jar empty.

2. **Measure** Put a thermometer in each jar. Read each thermometer. Record each temperature.

3. **Record Data** Put the jars in a sunny place. Record the temperatures every 30 minutes.

STEP 1

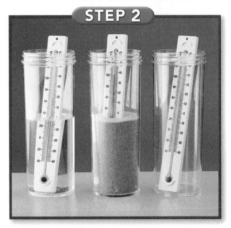

STEP 2

STEP 3

Think and Share

1. **Compare** Which jar had the warmest temperature after 90 minutes?

2. **Infer** Why was one jar warmer?

Guided Inquiry

Experiment Try the same experiment another day. Is your data the same as it was the first time? Why do you think that happened?

► **Vocabulary**

heat

◉ **Reading Skill**

Cause and Effect

GPS S1P1a. Recognize sources of light.

Heat

Heat makes things warm. Earth gets heat from the Sun. Earth gets light from the Sun, too.

The Sun warms Earth's air, water, and land. The Sun also warms you. You feel warm when you stand in a sunny place. You feel cooler in a shady place.

Heat comes from other places, too. Fire gives off heat. So do a lit stove, a burning candle, and a turned-on light bulb. Rubbing things together can make them give off heat, too.

▲ Be careful! Light bulbs get very hot.

▶ **Cause and Effect** What warms Earth's air, land, and water?

◀ Heat warms your home.

What happens when you rub your hands together? Try it! ▶

Heat Changes Things

Heat can make things change. Heat from your body makes your sheets warm. Heat from the Sun can make a metal slide too hot to use. Heat from a flame melts a candle. Heat makes butter soft.

▲ Heat makes ice melt.

▼ Heat cooks food.

A fire gives off heat when it burns. You feel the heat as the fire warms your body. Heat spreads out and warms things around it.

Heat can move things. Heat from flames moves the air. The air moves this windmill.

Heat can make things move. ▼

▶ **Cause and Effect** What are some ways that heat causes change?

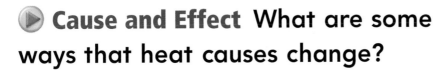

Lesson Wrap-Up

❶ **Vocabulary** What does **heat** do?

❷ **Reading Skill** How can heat from the Sun or a fire make your body feel different?

❸ **Measure** How can you measure to find out if heat changed the water in a pot on the stove?

📱 **Technology** Visit **www.eduplace.com/gascp** to find out more about heat.

Focus On

Readers' Theater

Cooking Contest

Cast

Judge

Chef 1

Chef 2

Chef 3

GPS **STANDARDS S1CS5a.** Describe and compare things in terms of number, shape, texture, size, weight, color, and motion.

READING LINK

Judge: Welcome to the Cooking Contest. Chef 1, tell me about what you made.

Chef 1: Judge, I made lasagna! I put hard noodles in hot water. The heat and the water made the noodles soft.

Judge: What did you do next?

Chef 1: I mixed liquid tomato sauce with the noodles. I added meat, cheese, and vegetables.

Judge: It sounds delicious! May I try a bite? [The judge tastes.] Yum! This is delicious.

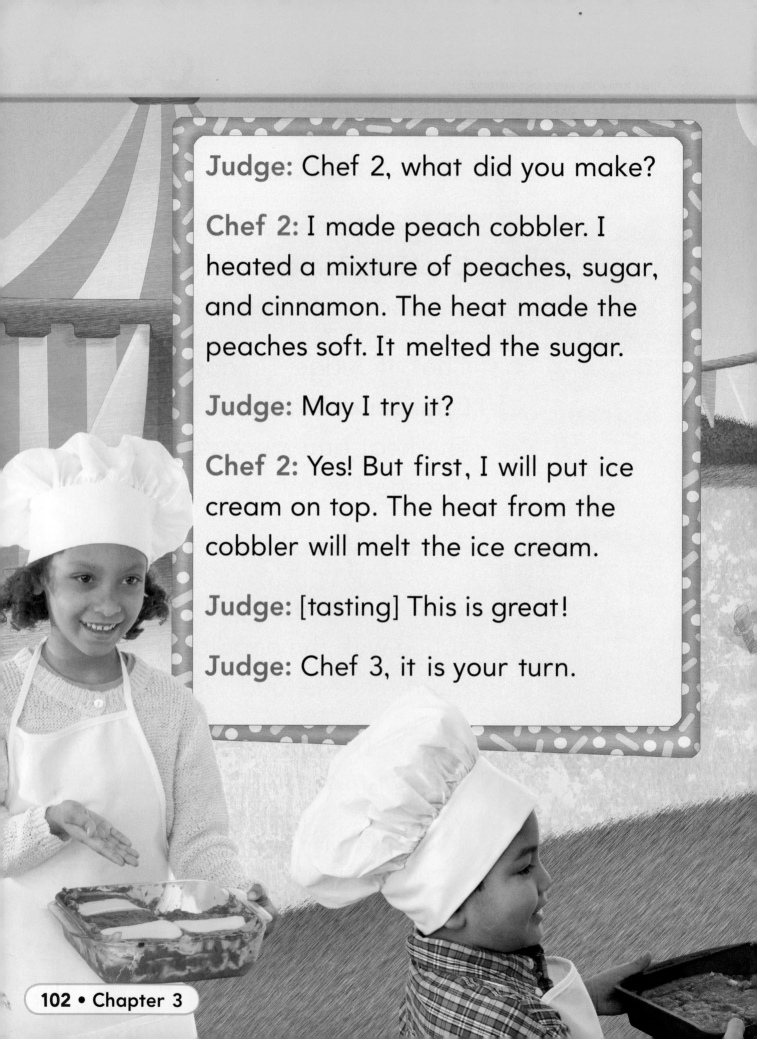

Judge: Chef 2, what did you make?

Chef 2: I made peach cobbler. I heated a mixture of peaches, sugar, and cinnamon. The heat made the peaches soft. It melted the sugar.

Judge: May I try it?

Chef 2: Yes! But first, I will put ice cream on top. The heat from the cobbler will melt the ice cream.

Judge: [tasting] This is great!

Judge: Chef 3, it is your turn.

Chef 3: I made cold green pea and mint soup.

Judge: I thought soups were hot.

Chef 3: The soup starts hot, but I cool it. I melt butter. Then I mix in onions, peas, mint, and milk. Last, I put the soup in the refrigerator. Have a taste.

Judge: What a mixture! Now, I must choose a winner.

Sharing Ideas

1. **Write About It** Choose a winner. List ways the winning chef used heating, cooling, and mixing.

2. **Talk About It** What is your favorite food? How do you use heating, cooling, and mixing to make it?

GEORGIA STANDARDS

S1CS6b. Science involves collecting data and testing hypotheses.
S1P1a. Recognize sources of light.

 Essential Question

Where Does Light Come From?

Science and You

A lighthouse helps ships find their way in the dark.

Inquiry Skill

Ask Questions You can ask questions to learn more about the world around you.

What You Need

objects

paper

tape

flashlight

Habi
of
Min

Shine Light

Steps

1 Tape paper to a wall. Shine light on the paper.

2 **Observe** Hold one object between the flashlight and the paper.

3 **Record Data** Write or draw what you see.

4 **Predict** Tell which objects you think light will pass through. Repeat steps 2 and 3 for each object.

STEP 1

STEP 2

STEP 3

Think and Share

1. How did your predictions compare to what happened?

2. **Classify** Group the objects by how light passes through them. Explain your groups.

Guided Inquiry

Ask Questions Complete this sentence: I wonder if light will pass through ___. Predict what will happen. Then try it. Share your results.

Vocabulary

light

shadow

▶ **Reading Skill**

**Main Idea
and Details**

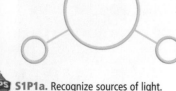

S1P1a. Recognize sources of light.

S1P1b. Explain how shadows are
made.

Light

You know that Earth gets heat from the Sun. Earth also gets light from the Sun. You can see **light**.

Things other than the Sun give off light, too. Fires, candles, and matches are things that burn. They give off light and heat.

The Sun gives off light.

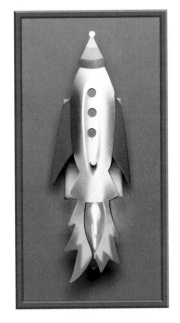

▲ night light

▲ fireworks

▲ firefly

Light bulbs give off light. When you bend a glow stick, it gives off light. Even some living things give off light.

▶ **Main Idea** Where does Earth get its light?

Express Lab

Activity Card 9
Make Shadows

Light and Shadows

Light can pass through some things but not others. Light passes through clear glass and clear plastic. It also passes through water and air.

What Light Passes Through

1 Light passes through.

2 Some light passes through.

3 No light passes through.

Other things stop some or all light from passing through. Wax paper and sunglasses block some light. Your body blocks all light. A dark shape called a **shadow** forms when something blocks light.

The boy and the dog block light from the Sun.

▶ **Main Idea** What is a shadow?

Lesson Wrap-Up

❶ **Vocabulary** What **lights** Earth?

❷ **Reading Skill** What are four things that give off light?

❸ **Ask Questions** What else do you want to know about light and shadows?

💻 **Technology** Visit **www.eduplace.com/gascp** to find out more about light.

STANDARDS S1P1c. Investigate how vibrations produce sound.

Echoes in the Dark

Can you use your ears to see? Bats do! They use sound to "see." They send out loud vibrations that human ears cannot hear. Like light, the sound vibration bounces off objects. Then the sound returns to the bat's big ears. This tells the bat where to find the objects.

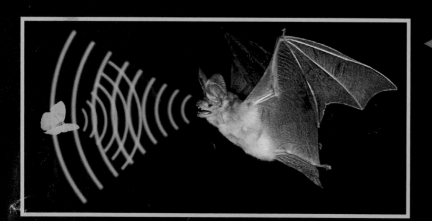

◀ Bats "see" and find an insect by bouncing sound vibrations off it.

▼ In the dark, the big ears of a bat act as its eyes. The bat's hearing is so good, it can tell where an insect is and how big it is.

111

GEORGIA STANDARDS

S1CS3c. Identify and practice accepted safety procedures in manipulating science materials and equipment.
S1P1c. Investigate how vibrations produce sound.

How Is Sound Made?

Science and You

Many living things use sound to communicate.

Inquiry Skill

Observe You can look and listen to learn about something.

What You Need

goggles

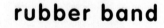

rubber band

can

Make Sounds

Steps

1 Stretch a rubber band around a can, across the open top. **Safety:** Wear goggles. Hold the rubber band carefully.

STEP 1

2 **Observe** Use your finger to pluck the rubber band. Look and listen closely.

STEP 2

3 **Record Data** Write about what you see and hear.

STEP 3

The rubber band

Think and Share

1. **Compare** How did the rubber band change when you plucked it?

2. **Infer** How do you think sound is made? Tell why.

Guided Inquiry

Solve a Problem Think of two ways to change the sound the rubber band makes. Then try them. Share your ways with the class.

113

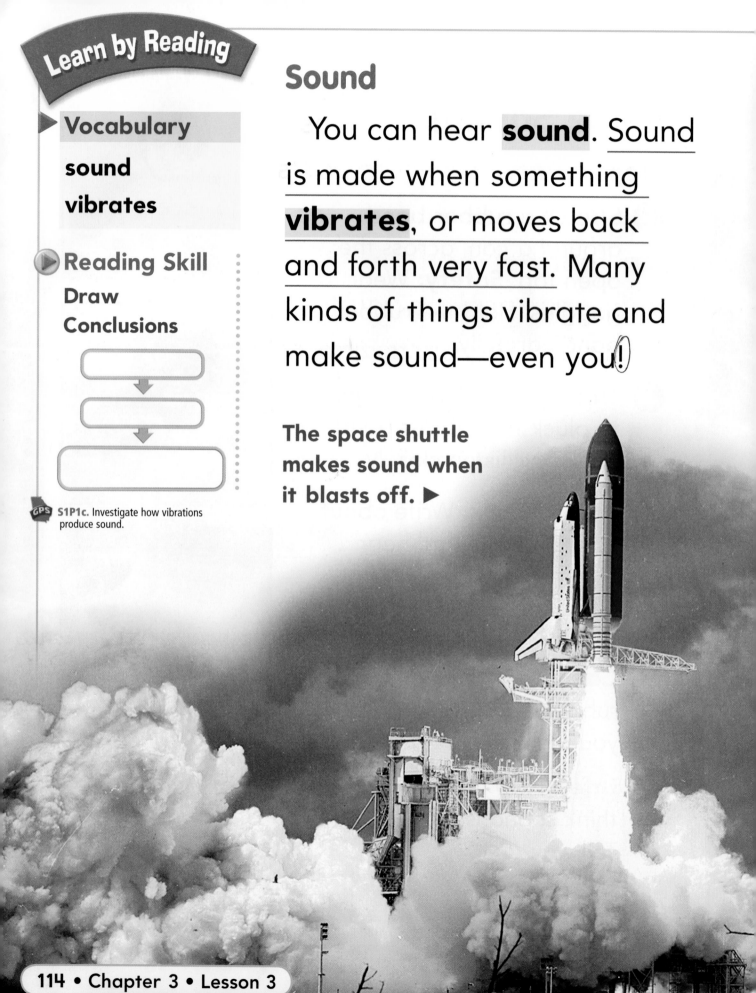

▶ **Vocabulary**

sound

vibrates

▶ **Reading Skill**

Draw
Conclusions

S1P1c. Investigate how vibrations produce sound.

Sound

You can hear **sound**. Sound is made when something **vibrates**, or moves back and forth very fast. Many kinds of things vibrate and make sound—even you!

The space shuttle makes sound when it blasts off. ▶

You make sound when you talk or sing. Sound happens when moving air makes parts inside your neck vibrate. Place your hand on the side of your neck as you talk. You can feel the parts vibrate.

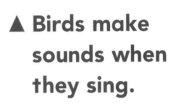

▲ **Birds make sounds when they sing.**

🔘 **Draw Conclusions** What causes sound when a bird sings?

Sound can be music. ▶

Express Lab

Activity Card 10
Listen for Sounds

Hearing Sound

A drum vibrates when you strike it. Something that vibrates makes air around it vibrate, too. Air that vibrates makes parts inside your ears vibrate. Then you hear sound.

▶ **Draw Conclusions** How does the sound of a drum reach your ears?

Lesson Wrap-Up

❶ **Vocabulary** How is **sound** made?

❷ **Reading Skill** How do you think a guitar string makes a sound?

❸ **Observe** If you see something vibrate, what will you hear?

🖥 **Technology** Visit www.eduplace.com/gascp to find out more about sound.

 STANDARDS S1P1c. Investigate how vibrations produce sound.

Thump, Thump

A doctor uses a stethoscope to hear sounds inside your body. Part of the stethoscope vibrates when your heart beats. Vibrations go through tubes on the stethoscope to the doctor's ears.

 **Sharing Ideas**

1. **Write About It** Draw a stethoscope. Write about how sound moves in it.

2. **Talk About It** Talk about questions that you can ask doctors about what they hear through stethoscopes.

Lesson 4

GPS **GEORGIA STANDARDS**

S1CS6b. Science involves collecting data and testing hypotheses.
S1P1d. Differentiate between various sounds in terms of (pitch) high or low and (volume) loud or soft.

? How Are Sounds Different?

Science and You

Sometimes people use sounds to make music.

Inquiry Skill

Use Data Compare what you learn to find patterns.

What You Need

5 jars

water

pencil

paper

Habi
of
Min

Different Sounds

Steps

1. Pour different amounts of water into four jars. Leave one jar empty.

2. **Observe** Tap the side of each jar with a pencil. Listen to the sounds.

3. **Record Data** Write letters to order the jars from the lowest sound to the highest sounds.

STEP 1

STEP 2

STEP 3

Think and Share

1. **Use Data** Which jar made the lowest sound? Which made the highest sound? How much water was in those jars?

2. **Infer** How does the amount of water affect the sound?

Guided Inquiry

Be an Inventor Hum a song. Use the jars to play the song. Add more jars and water if you need them. Then have a class concert.

119

▶ Vocabulary

pitch
volume

▶ Reading Skill

Compare and Contrast

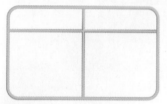

GPS **S1P1d.** Differentiate between various sounds in terms of (pitch) high or low and (volume) loud or soft.

S1P1e. Identify emergency sounds and sounds that help us stay safe.

Pitch and Volume

Not all sounds are the same. **Pitch** is how high or low a sound is. The faster something vibrates, the higher the sound it makes. Fast vibrations cause a high pitch. Slow vibrations cause a low pitch.

violin with high pitch ▼

bass with low pitch ▶

Express Lab

Activity Card 11
Make Sounds

120

Volume is how loud or soft a sound is. When you whisper, you use a little energy to make a soft sound. When you yell, you use a lot of energy to make a loud sound.

▶ **Compare and Contrast**
How is a high pitch different from a low pitch?

loud volume ▲

▼ soft volume

▲ Smoke alarms beep when something is burning.

Sounds Keep You Safe

Some sounds are warnings that keep you safe. They warn you to get out of the way or to go to a safe place.

Sirens warn drivers to get out of the way.

Lesson Wrap-Up

1. **Vocabulary** What is **volume**?

2. **Reading Skill** Compare loud and soft sounds.

3. **Use Data** What does how fast or slow something vibrates tell about pitch?

Technology Visit **www.eduplace.com/gascp** to find out more about sound.

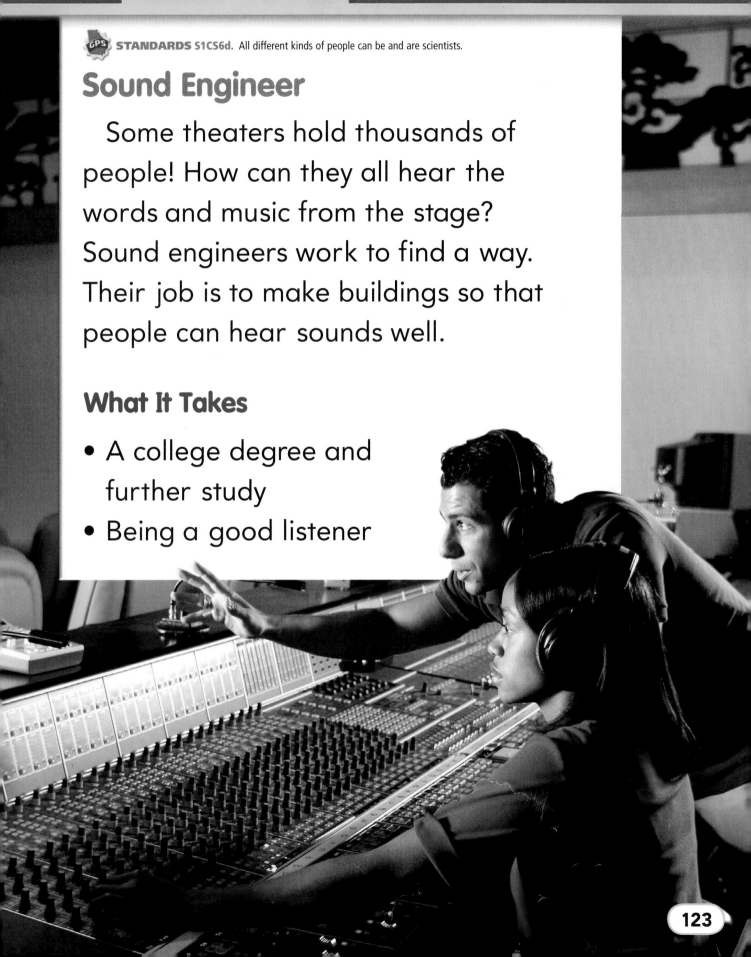

Careers in Science

STANDARDS S1CS6d. All different kinds of people can be and are scientists.

Sound Engineer

Some theaters hold thousands of people! How can they all hear the words and music from the stage? Sound engineers work to find a way. Their job is to make buildings so that people can hear sounds well.

What It Takes

- A college degree and further study
- Being a good listener

LINKS
for Home and School

 STANDARDS M1G3. Students will arrange and describe objects in space proximity, position, and direction (near, far, below, above, up, down, behind, in front of, next to, and left or right of). **GeorgiaTask S1P1H**

Math Find a Sound

Work with four classmates. Give each classmate a bell. Put on a blindfold. Look at the picture to see how to stand.

When one classmate rings a bell, use the words **left**, **right**, **front**, or **back** to tell where you heard the sound.

 **Loud or Soft Sounds**

Make a list of loud sounds and soft sounds. Circle the ones that you do not like because they are too loud.

Performance Task

GeorgiaTask S1P1B

What sounds do you hear?

You hear many sounds every day. How are they different?

- Use a tape recorder to make a tape of school sounds.

- Have a partner listen to the tape and sort the sounds into different groups.

- List the sounds you like and sounds you do not like.

Visual Summary

Some objects give off heat, light, or sound.

Heat	Light	Sound
Heat makes things warm	You can see light	You can hear sound

Main Ideas

1. **What are three things that give off light?**
   (pp. 106–107) *light bolb sun TV* S1P1a

2. **Tell how shadows are made.** (pp. 108–109) S1P1b

3. **How are pitch and volume different?**
   (pp. 120–121) *Shadows are made from the sun its like but its block* S1P1d

4. **What are two things that make sounds to keep you safe?** (p. 122) *fire truck and paice officer.* S1P1e

Vocabulary

Choose the correct word from the box.

S1CS7a

5. It makes things warm

6. How high or low a sound is

7. You can see it

8. Moves back and forth very fast

heat (p. 96)
light (p. 106)
pitch (p. 120)
vibrates (p. 114)

Using Science Skills

9. **Observe** When will you see a shadow? S1P1b

10. **Critical Thinking** How can you tell there is sound if you cannot hear it? S1P1c

GPS CRCT Prep

Choose a word to complete the sentence.

11. When an object blocks light, a _____ is formed.

  light   shadow   sound
   Ⓐ   Ⓑ   Ⓒ   S1P1b

Chapter 4

Magnets

Groceries
eggs
milk
bread

Baseball
Game at
6:00 PM

Refrigerator magnets

LESSON 1 A magnet pulls paper clips and other objects toward it. Why does this happen?

LESSON 2  The iron filings make a pattern around a magnet. Where is a magnet's force strongest?

LESSON 3 Magnets can make things move without touching them. How do you think this happens?

Vocabulary Preview

Vocabulary

Vocabulary Skill

Use Opposites

attract

repel

These words are opposites. **Attract** means to pull toward. What do you think repel means?

attract
When objects attract, they pull toward each other.

poles
The poles are the places on a magnet where the forces are strongest.

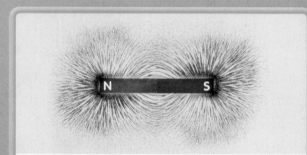

magnetic field
The space around a magnet where the magnet's force works.

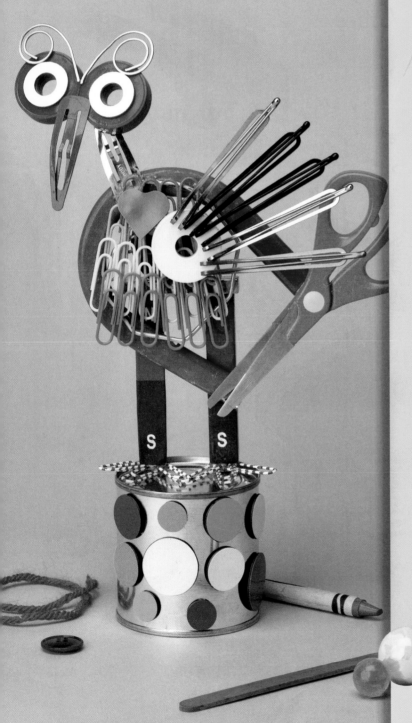

magnetic
If an object and a magnet attract each other, the object is magnetic.

Start with Your Standards

Habits of Mind

S1CS3a. Use ordinary hand tools and instruments to construct, measure, and look at objects.

The Nature of Science

S1CS6c. Scientists often repeat experiments multiple times, and subject their ideas to criticism by other scientists who may disagree with them and do further tests.

Physical Science

S1P2a. Demonstrate how magnets attract and repel.

S1P2b. Identify common objects that are attracted to a magnet.

S1P2c. Identify objects and materials (air, water, wood, paper, your hand, etc.) that do not block magnetic force.

GPS GEORGIA STANDARDS

S1CS6c. Scientists often repeat experiments multiple times, and subject their ideas to criticism by other scientists who may disagree with them and do further tests.
S1P2a. Demonstrate how magnets attract and repel.

? What Are Magnets?

Science and You

Magnets can pull toward each other or push away from each other.

Inquiry Skill

Observe Use your senses and tools to find out about something.

What You Need

2 bar magnets

Habits of Mind

Test Magnets

Steps

1. **Observe** Hold an end of one magnet near an end of the other magnet.

2. **Record Data** Write your observations on a chart.

3. **Experiment** Turn one magnet around. Hold it near the other magnet. Write what happened.

4. Turn the other magnet around. Write what happened.

STEP 1

STEP 2

Testing Magnets

Position of the Magnets	What Happened
1.	
2.	
3.	

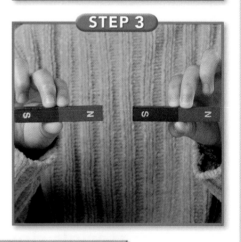

STEP 3

Think and Share

1. **Compare** When was the push or pull stronger?

2. How do magnets act on each other?

Guided Inquiry

Experiment What if you repeat the activity with horseshoe magnets? Predict what will happen. Then try it and share your results with others.

magnet
attract
magnetic
poles
repels

▶ **Reading Skill**

Cause and Effect

S1P2a. Demonstrate how magnets attract and repel.

S1P2b. Identify common objects that are attracted to a magnet.

Which materials does the magnet attract?

Magnets

A **magnet** is an object that attracts iron or steel objects. When objects **attract**, they pull toward each other. If an object and a magnet attract each other, the object is **magnetic**.

Not all objects are magnetic. Objects made from glass, wood, plastic, or paper are not magnetic.

▶ **Cause and Effect**
Why are some objects attracted by a magnet?

magnetic objects

These objects are not magnetic.

Express Lab

Activity Card 12
Observe Magnets

Magnets Act on Each Other

All magnets have forces that push or pull on other magnets. All magnets have two poles. The **poles** are the places on a magnet where the forces are strongest.

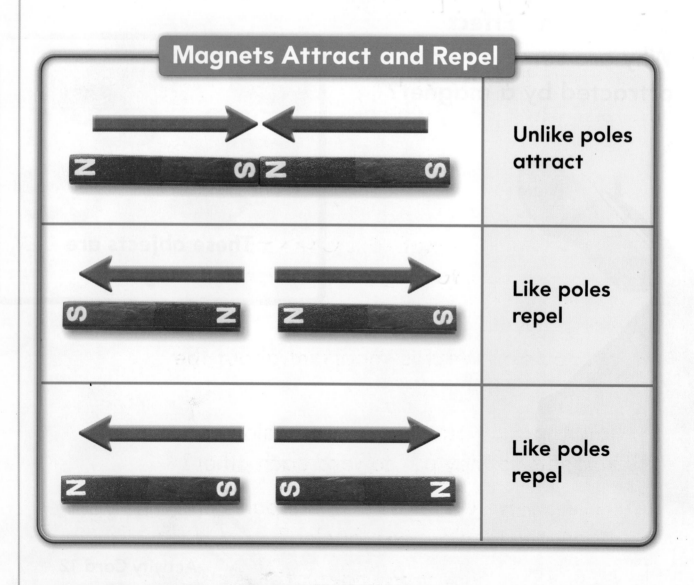

Magnets Attract and Repel

N — S N — S	Unlike poles attract
← S N N — S →	Like poles repel
← N S S N →	Like poles repel

If two unlike poles are near each other, the magnets attract. If two like poles are near each other, the magnets repel. When a magnet **repels**, it pushes an object away from itself.

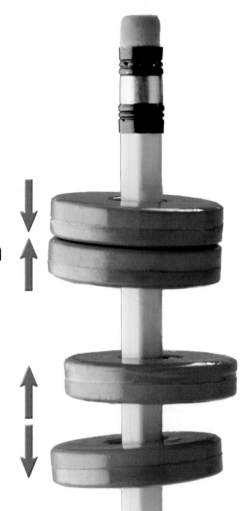

▶ **Cause and Effect** What happens when like poles are together?

What causes the magnets to be in this position?

Lesson Wrap-Up

❶ **Vocabulary** What is important about the **poles** of a magnet?

❷ **Reading Skill** How should you hold two magnets so they pull toward each other?

❸ **Observe** How can you find the poles of a magnet if they are not labeled?

🖥 **Technology** Visit **www.eduplace.com/gascp** to find out more about magnets.

Maglev Trains

Scientists have used magnets to build a new kind of train. The push and pull of magnets move the maglev train. The pulling force of the magnet causes the train to float up to four inches above the track!

The maglev train moves twice as fast as other trains.

Magnets cause the train to move forward without touching the track. Magnets in the front of the train pull it. Magnets behind the train push it.

Magnetic coils along the track attract magnets on the train. The coils and magnets never touch.

Magnetic coils in the track

Magnets on the maglev train

Sharing Ideas

1. **Write About It** What causes the maglev to move forward?

2. **Talk About It** How did scientists help people by inventing the maglev?

GPS **GEORGIA STANDARDS**

S1CS1a. Raise questions about the world around them and be willing to seek answers to some of the questions by making careful observations and measurements and trying to figure things out.
S1P2a. Demonstrate how magnets attract and repel.

? Essential Question
What Is a Magnetic Field?

Science and You

Iron filings can show where the force of a magnet is strongest.

Inquiry Skill

Infer Use what you observe and know to tell what you think.

What You Need

goggles

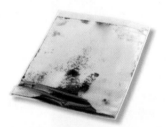

filings

bar magnet

Filing Patterns

Steps

1 **Safety:** Wear goggles! Place filings on top of a bar magnet.

STEP 1

2 **Observe** Look at the pattern that the filings make. Draw what you see.

STEP 2

3 **Record Data** Move the filings on top of the magnet. Draw what you see.

4 What will you see if you move the filings again? Test your prediction.

STEP 3

Think and Share

1. **Infer** Why does the pattern change when you move the filings?

2. Which part of the magnet attracted the most filings? Tell why.

Guided Inquiry

Ask Questions Finish this question. How would the pattern look if I used a _____ magnet? Work together with a partner to find out.

GPS **S1P2a.** Demonstrate how magnets attract and repel.

Magnetic Fields

The space around a magnet where the magnet's force works is a **magnetic field**. A magnet can attract or repel only the objects in its magnetic field.

You cannot see a magnetic field. You can find it by placing iron filings around a magnet.

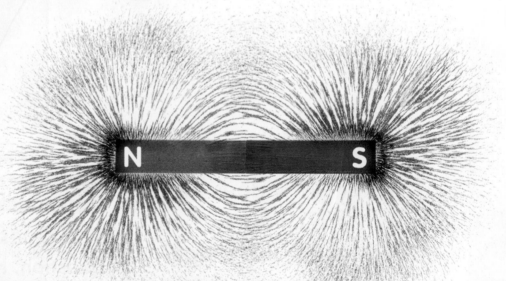

The iron filings show that the magnetic field is strongest at the poles.

Express Lab

Activity Card 13
Observe a Magnetic Field

A magnet's force is strongest at its poles. The force is strong enough to push or pull objects, even without touching them.

▶ **Compare and Contrast** How is the center of a magnet different from the poles?

Magnetic objects are pulled to the poles at the ends of this magnet.

Lesson Wrap-Up

① **Vocabulary** What is a **magnetic field**?

② **Reading Skill** Why do objects hang from the ends of a bar magnet and not from the middle?

③ **Infer** What can you infer about a magnet by looking at a pattern of iron filings around it?

🖳 **Technology** Visit **www.eduplace.com/gascp** to find out more about magnetic fields.

EXTREME Science

MAGNET POWER!

What zooms this roller coaster to the speed of a car in just four seconds? Not a motor! Magnetic force does it. Strong magnets along the track attract and repel the cars without touching them.

Hold on! The strong magnets of this roller coaster will soon rocket these riders 150 feet into the air!

GEORGIA STANDARDS

S1CS3a. Use ordinary hand tools and instruments to construct, measure, and look at objects.
S1P2c. Identify objects and materials (air, water, wood, paper, your hand, etc.) that do not block magnetic force.

How Strong Is a Magnet's Force?

Essential Question

Science and You

A magnet's force can attract objects without touching them.

Inquiry Skill

Predict Use patterns you observe to tell what you think will happen.

What You Need

magnet

paper clip on a string

tape

construction paper

Observe Force

Steps

1 Hang a paper clip from a table with string and tape.

2 **Experiment** Wave a magnet under the clip. Observe. Lower the magnet. Wave it again. Lower the magnet. Observe.

3 **Predict** Repeat Step 2. Have a partner put paper between the magnet and the clip. What will happen to the clip? Try it.

STEP 1

STEP 2

STEP 3

Think and Share

1. What made the paper clip move?

2. **Infer** Where does a magnet's force get weaker?

Habits of Mind

Guided Inquiry

Experiment Find out if a magnet's force is changed by temperature. Make a plan and try it out. Communicate your results.

▶ **Vocabulary**

magnetic force

▶ **Reading Skill**

Draw Conclusions

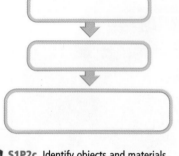

GPS **S1P2c.** Identify objects and materials (air, water, wood, paper, your hand, etc.) that do not block magnetic force.

Magnets Work from a Distance

Magnetic force is the pushing or pulling force of a magnet. Magnetic force can make an object move without touching it. Magnetic force pushes the like poles of two magnets away from one another.

Magnets work through air.

Magnets work through paper.

A magnet's force can attract objects through other materials. A magnet's force may work through paper, glass, plastic, water, and air.

Magnets work through plastic.

Draw Conclusions How can a magnet hold a picture to a refrigerator?

Magnets work through glass and water.

Express Lab

Activity Card 14
Move Objects with Magnets

Weakening a Magnet's Force

<u>Magnetic force gets weaker as an object moves away from a magnet.</u> The object is moving away from the magnetic field.

A strong magnet has a larger magnetic field. A strong magnet can attract an object from farther away.

▶ **Draw Conclusions** Why won't a weak magnet work through wood?

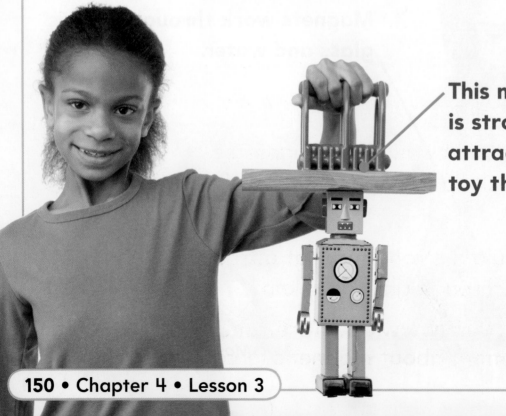

This magnet's force is strong. It can attract the heavy toy through wood.

Magnetic Force

The magnet attracts many pins. Its magnetic force passes through one sheet of paper.

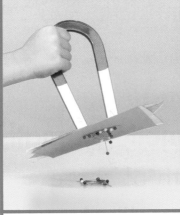

More paper has been added. The pins are farther away from the magnet's poles. The magnet's force is weaker.

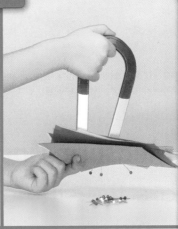

More paper has been added. The pins are even farther from the magnet. Now the force is too weak to hold them.

Lesson Wrap-Up

❶ **Vocabulary** What is **magnetic force**?

❷ **Reading Skill** Why might a magnet be unable to pick up a magnetic object from a distance?

❸ **Predict** Could a strong magnet attract an iron object through glass? Explain.

Technology Visit **www.eduplace.com/gascp** to find out more about magnetic force.

STANDARDS S1CS2d. Make quantitative estimates of familiar lengths, weights, and time intervals, and check them by measuring.
ELA1W1b. Describes an experience in writing.

Math Measure Magnetic Strength

Compare the strength of three magnets. Place a paper clip next to a magnet. Move the clip until the magnet no longer attracts it. Estimate and measure the distance. Which magnet has the strongest force?

Magnet	Distance

 **Describe an Event**

Write about a magnet used to make something move. Tell what happened first, next, and last.

Georgia

GeorgiaTask S1P2B

How can magnets move objects?

Magnets can make some things move without touching them. Find out how.

- Put paper clips in a cup.

- Hold a magnet over the cup.

- Record what happens.

- Hold a magnet near the side of the cup.

- Record what happens.

Careers in Science

 STANDARDS S1CS6d. All different kinds of people can be and are scientists.

Computer Scientist

Today's computers are smaller, faster, and more useful than before. Computer scientists made this happen. They make new computers and help people use them.

Did you know that computers use magnets? Tiny magnets help a computer store information.

What It Takes

- A college degree in computer science
- Math and communication skills

People in Science

Dr. Bamidele Kammen

Meet Dr. Bamidele Kammen. She is a radiologist. A radiologist uses machines to take pictures of the inside of a person's body.

One of the machines uses magnets. Another machine uses X-rays. Later, Dr. Kammen looks at the pictures to see if all is well inside a person.

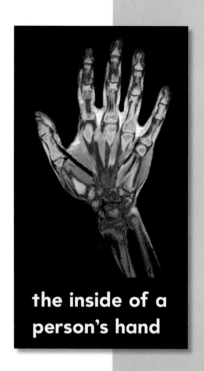

the inside of a person's hand

Visual Summary

Magnets attract objects made of iron or steel. They can move some objects without touching them.

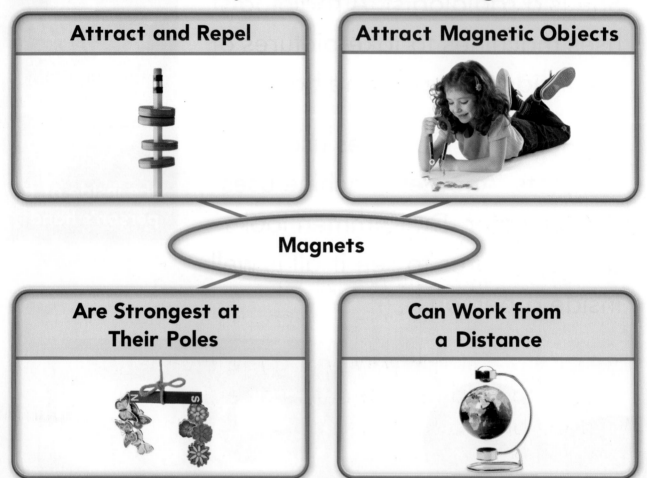

Attract and Repel

Attract Magnetic Objects

Magnets

Are Strongest at Their Poles

Can Work from a Distance

Main Ideas

1. What can the magnetic force of one magnet do to another magnet? (p. 136) `S1P2a`

2. Where on a magnet is the force strongest? (p. 143) `S1P2a`

Vocabulary

Choose the correct word from the box.

3. An object that is attracted by a magnet

4. Pushes an object away from itself

5. To pull toward each other

> **S1CS7a**
> **attract** (p. 134)
> **magnetic** (p. 134)
> **repels** (p. 137)

Using Science Skills

6. Predict what will happen if you put a magnet near a pile of steel paper clips. **S1P2b**

7. **Critical Thinking** Why might a magnet be able to hold one object to a refrigerator door but not another? **S1P2c**

GPS CRCT Prep

8. A magnet's force is strongest at

   its poles.   its middle.   one end.

    Ⓐ   Ⓑ   Ⓒ   **S1P2a**

GPS Test Practice

Choose the correct answer.

1. Which is our main source of light?

    the Sun   the Earth   the Moon
      Ⓐ   Ⓑ   Ⓒ

   `S1P1a`

2. Which object will not make a shadow?

    your hand   clear glass   a book
      Ⓐ   Ⓑ   Ⓒ

   `S1P1b`

3. Which object is most likely not magnetic?

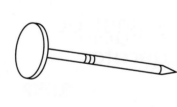      

      Ⓐ   Ⓑ   Ⓒ

   `S1P2b`

4. Sound is made when an object

    vibrates.   gets shorter.   gets longer.
      Ⓐ   Ⓑ   Ⓒ

   `S1P1c`

5. Which would make the best warning sound?

low pitch, high pitch, low pitch,
soft volume loud volume loud volume

(A) (B) (C)

S1P1d
S1P1e

6. Which would block the magnetic force of a weak magnet?

water thin paper thick wood

(A) (B) (C)

S1P2c

GPS Checking Main Ideas

Write the correct answer.

7. You move a magnet under a table. Paper clips on top of the table move. Why?

S1P2a

8. Describe the pitch and volume of the sounds these animals make.

S1P1d

You Can...

Discover More

How can you hear music through a wall?

Sound travels. Music can travel through a wall. The music moves out from the object that made the sound. Then it moves through the air and the wall to your ear.

 Go to **www.eduplace.com/gascp** to make sound waves travel.

GEORGIA UNIT C SCIENCE

Life Science

Cricket Connection

Visit www.eduplace.com/gascp to check out *Click, Ask,* and *Odyssey* magazine articles and activities.

Life Science

Independent Reading

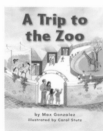

Living
Things

A Trip to
the Zoo

The Venus
Flytrap

 Fun Facts

Loggerhead turtles
swim for years and
travel over 9,000 miles.

Life Science

Plants and animals meet their needs in different ways.

Georgia Aquarium in Atlanta, Georgia

GPS STANDARDS ELA1R6a. Reads and listens to a variety of texts for information and pleasure.

A Dragonfly

by Eleanor Farjeon

When the heat of the summer
Made drowsy the land,
A dragonfly came
And sat on my hand.

With its blue-jointed body,
And wings like spun glass,
It lit on my fingers
As though they were grass.

Science in Georgia

GPS **STANDARDS S1L1d.** Compare and describe various animals—appearance, motion, growth, basic needs.

Who Lives in the Forest?

All these animals live in Georgia, just like you.

Night Hunter!
The bobcat lives in forests and swamps. Rabbits and woodchucks need to stay safe when this cat is hungry!

Woodchucks use their strong legs to dig dens under ground.

Rabbits hide in bushes when danger is near.

Science in Georgia

GPS STANDARDS S1L1d. Compare and describe various animals—appearance, motion, growth, basic needs.

Baby Bobcats

A bobcat mother has two kittens in the spring. She has to care for them by giving them food and shelter.

Safe at Home

A mother bobcat uses a rocky ledge to keep her babies safe and warm.

New Hunter

Mother bobcats bring small, live animals back to the den. Then the kittens can practice hunting.

Choose a word to complete the sentence.

1. Bobcats hunt at <u>morning</u>

   Ⓐ day.

   Ⓑ night.

   Ⓒ morning.

   S1L1d

 Performance Task

Animal Home

Draw a picture of an animal and its home. Write a sentence about how its home keeps the animal safe. Share your work with a partner.

S1L1b

STANDARDS S1CS7d. Much can be learned about plants and animals by observing them closely, but care must be taken to know the needs of living things and how to provide for them. Advantage can be taken of classroom pets.
GeorgiaTask S1L1E

Observe an Animal

How can you find out what an animal needs to live and grow? Watch an animal. Write and draw what you see.

What You Need

• animals

Step 1: Plan

- Choose an animal to observe.

Step 2: Do It

- **Observe** the animal. Watch it each day.

- **Record** what you see. Draw pictures to show how the animal finds food and shelter.

Step 3: Share

- Use your pictures to make a book. Write about how the animal finds what it needs to stay alive. Share your book with other groups.

Chapter 5

Plants

LESSON 1

Strawberries are plants. What do plants need to grow?

LESSON 2

Buttercups have flowers and leaves. What are other plant parts?

LESSON 3

A plant's roots are below the ground. What do roots do?

LESSON 4

Leaves grow toward light. Why does this happen?

Vocabulary Preview

Vocabulary

Vocabulary Skill

Break It Apart

sunlight

Find the two smaller words in this word. Say each word. Then say the words together.

leaves

Leaves are parts of a plant that make food for the plant.

roots

Roots are the parts of a plant that take in water from the ground.

soil

Soil is the loose top layer of Earth.

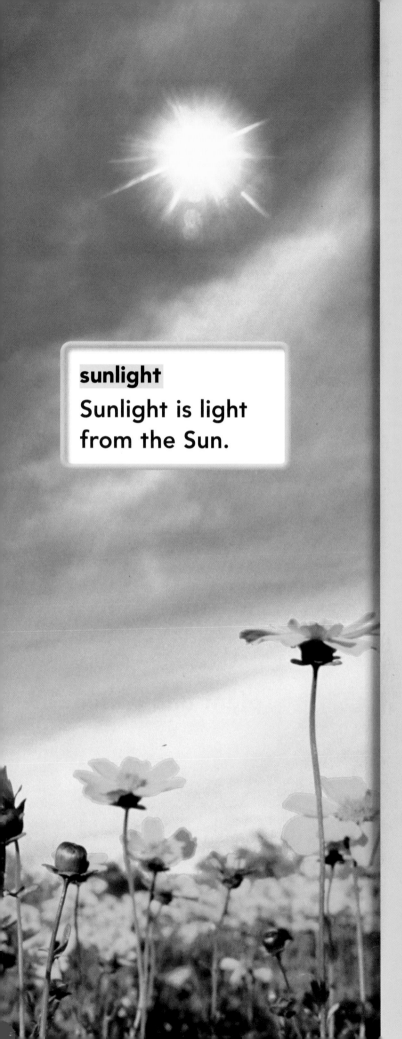

sunlight

Sunlight is light from the Sun.

Start with Your Standards

Habits of Mind

S1CS4b. Describe changes in the size, weight, color, or movement of things, and note which of their other qualities remain the same during a specific change.

S1CS5b. Draw pictues (grade level appropriate) that correctly portray features of the thing being described.

S1CS5c. Use simple pictographs and bar graphs to communicate data.

The Nature of Science

S1CS7d. Much can be learned about plants and animals by observing them closely, but care must be taken to know the needs of living things and how to provide for them. Advantage can be taken of classroom pets.

Life Science

S1L1a. Identify the basic needs of a plant.
1. Air
2. Water
3. Light
4. Nutrients

S1L1c. Identify the parts of a plant—root, stem, leaf, and flower.

Lesson 1

GEORGIA STANDARDS

S1CS3a. Use ordinary hand tools and instruments to construct, measure, and look at objects.
S1L1a. Identify the basic needs of a plant.
1. Air; 2. Water; 3. Light; 4. Nutrients

Essential Question

What Are the Needs of Plants?

Science and You

Plants need water, light, air, and space to grow.

Inquiry Skill

Measure Use a tool to find how much or how many.

What You Need

goggles

ruler

plant and water

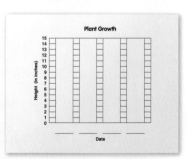

bar graph

Observe a Plant

Steps

1 **Measure** Use a ruler to measure a plant.
Safety: Wear goggles!

2 **Record Data** Record the height on a bar graph.

3 Keep the plant in a sunny place. Water the plant when needed.
Safety: Clean up spills!

4 **Measure** Each week, measure the plant again. Record the height.

STEP 1

STEP 2

STEP 3

Think and Share

1. **Compare** How did your graph compare with your classmates' graphs?

2. **Infer** What do plants need?

Guided Inquiry

Experiment Use what you know to predict how often you need to water a plant. Make a plan to check your prediction.

Habits of Mind

▶ **Vocabulary**

sunlight

▶ **Reading Skill**
**Compare and
Contrast**

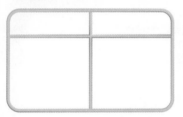

GPS **S1L1a.** Identify the basic needs
of a plant. 1. Air; 2. Water; 3. Light;
4. Nutrients

Needs of Plants

Plants need water, light, air, and space to live. Most plants get light from the Sun. Light from the Sun is called **sunlight**.

Some plants need a lot of light. Other plants do not need much light.

A healthy plant gets enough light, water, air, and space.

Which plant is not getting enough water?

Some plants need more water than other plants. A plant's leaves may sag if they do not get enough water. You can grow healthy plants if you know what they need.

▶ **Compare and Contrast** How are the needs of plants alike?

Express Lab

Activity Card 15
Design a Garden

Space to Grow

Plants need space to get the air, sunlight, and water they need. Large plants need a lot of space to grow. Small plants do not need as much space as large plants.

Big trees need more space than small flowers.

Plants that do not have enough space may not grow very big. After you plant a garden, you may need to take out some plants. That will give the other plants more space.

Plants need space to grow.

▶ **Compare and Contrast** How are the needs of large plants and small plants different?

Lesson Wrap-Up

❶ **Vocabulary** What is **sunlight**?

❷ **Reading Skill** What are some ways that the needs of plants are different?

❸ **Measure** How can measuring a plant tell you if it is getting what it needs?

🔦**Technology** Visit **www.eduplace.com/gascp** to find out more about the needs of plants.

179

Plants and Machines

Many people grow plants for food. Farmers use machines to give plants what they need to grow.

Some places do not get enough rain. Then farmers use machines to water the plants.

Machines water plants.

Sometimes people grow plants indoors. They use lights because the plants do not get enough sunlight to grow.

Lights help plants grow.

Sharing Ideas

1. **Write About It** How do farmers use machines to give plants what they need to grow?

2. **Talk About It** What are some different tools for watering plants?

Lesson 2

GEORGIA STANDARDS

S1CS5b. Draw pictures (grade level appropriate) that correctly portray features of the thing being described.

S1L1c. Identify the parts of a plant—root, stem, leaf, and flower.

What Are the Parts of Plants?

Science and You

Plants have different parts that help them get what they need to live.

Inquiry Skill

Compare Look for ways that objects are alike and different.

What You Need

goggles and paper towels

hand lens

2 plants

paper and crayons

Compare Plant Parts

Steps

1 Take both plants out of their pots. Carefully shake the dirt from the roots. **Safety:** Wear goggles!

STEP 1

2 **Observe** Use a hand lens. Look closely at the parts of each plant.

3 **Record data** Draw pictures to show the parts of each plant.

STEP 2

4 Put the plants back in the pots. **Safety:** Wash your hands!

STEP 3

Think and Share

1. **Compare** What parts do both plants have?

2. **Compare** How are the plants different?

Guided Inquiry

Ask Questions Find a gardener who can answer your questions about different plant parts. **Communicate** what you find.

Habits of Mind

Vocabulary

flower

leaves

stem

roots

▶ **Reading Skill**
Classify

GPS **S1L1c.** Identify the parts of a plant—root, stem, leaf, and flower.

Plant Parts

Plants have parts. Most plants have roots, stems, and leaves. Some plants have flowers. Each part helps the plant in a different way.

Express Lab

Activity Card 16
Be a Plant Expert

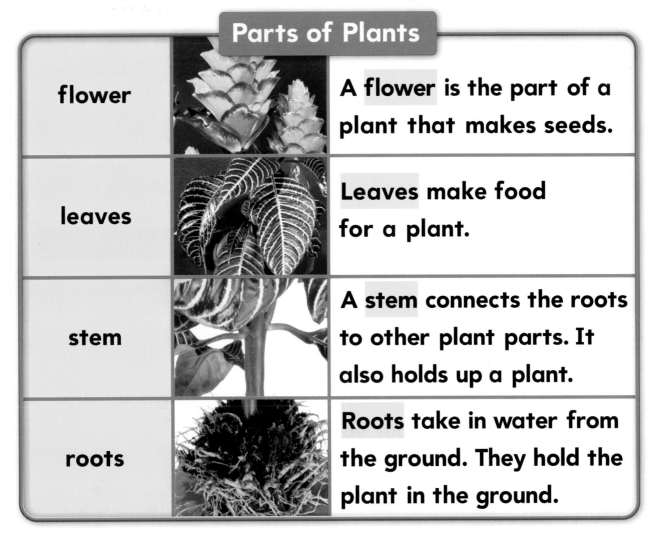

Parts of Plants

flower		A **flower** is the part of a plant that makes seeds.
leaves		**Leaves** make food for a plant.
stem		A **stem** connects the roots to other plant parts. It also holds up a plant.
roots		**Roots** take in water from the ground. They hold the plant in the ground.

▶ **Classify** Which part of the plant makes food?

Lesson Wrap-Up

❶ **Vocabulary** What are the parts of a plant?

❷ **Reading Skill** Which part of a plant holds the plant in the ground?

❸ **Compare** How are plants alike?

💻 **Technology** Visit **www.eduplace.com/gascp** to find out more about plant parts.

Lesson 3

GPS **GEORGIA STANDARDS**

S1CS4b. Describe changes in size, weight, color, or movement of things, and note which of their qualities remain the same during a specific change. **S1L1c.** Identify the parts of a plant—root, stem, leaf, and flower.

? How Do Roots Help Plants?

Essential Question

Science and You

A plant's roots take in water and nutrients from the soil.

Inquiry Skill

Infer Use what you observe and know to tell what you think.

What You Need

goggles and scissors

2 plants

roots   no roots

labels

water

Habits of Mind

What Roots Do

Steps

1. **Experiment** Cut the roots off one plant. **Safety:** Wear goggles. Scissors are sharp!

2. Put the stem back in soil. Label the plant **no roots. Safety:** Wash your hands!

3. Label the other plant **roots**. Put the plants in a sunny place. Water them. Observe them for a week.

4. **Record Data** Write about how each plant changed.

STEP 1

STEP 2

STEP 3

Think and Share

1. How did each plant change?

2. **Infer** What do roots do for a plant?

Guided Inquiry

Experiment Cut the leaves off a new plant. Predict what will happen after one week. Check your prediction.

Vocabulary

soil

nutrients

▶ **Reading Skill**

Main Idea and Details

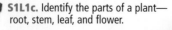

GPS **S1L1c.** Identify the parts of a plant— root, stem, leaf, and flower.

How Roots Work

The roots of most plants grow in soil. **Soil** is the loose top layer of Earth. **Nutrients** are materials in soil that plants need to grow. A plant's roots take in water and nutrients from the soil.

Water and nutrients move from the roots to other plant parts.

soil without plants

soil with plants

Roots help hold up a plant. They also help keep the soil in place. Soil can wash away when there are no plants.

▶ **Main Idea** How do roots help a plant?

Express Lab

Activity Card 17
Watch Water in a Plant

189

Different Kinds of Roots

Different plants have different kinds of roots. A dandelion has a long main root. Grass has many small roots. A tree has large roots that hold it in the ground.

This plant has many small roots.

These roots take in nutrients near the top of the soil.

Some plants have roots that people and animals eat. Carrots and radishes are roots.

▶ **Main Idea** What are some ways that roots look different?

People eat beet roots.

roots

Lesson Wrap-Up

❶ **Vocabulary** How does a plant get **nutrients**?

❷ **Reading Skill** What are two different kinds of roots?

❸ **Infer** What could happen to a plant if its roots were not in soil?

Technology Visit www.eduplace.com/gascp to find out more about plants.

EXTREME Science

Super Leaf

This leaf is so big you can sit in it like a boat! The Victoria water lily has the largest leaves of any plant on Earth. Some Victoria lily pads grow to more than two meters across! That's wider than a grown-up is tall.

A two-meter lily pad could easily float a hundred frogs without sinking!

Victoria water lilies need lots of sunlight and very warm weather to grow so big.

GEORGIA STANDARDS

S1CS7d. Much can be learned about plants and animals by observing them closely, but care must be taken to know the needs of living things and how to provide for them. Advantage can be taken of classroom pets.
S1L1a. Identify the basic needs of a plant. 1. Air; 2. Water; 3. Light; 4. Nutrients

Essential Question

How Do Leaves Help Plants?

Science and You

Leaves take in sunlight to make food for a plant. The plant needs food to grow.

Inquiry Skill

Experiment Make a plan, choosing the items to use and the steps to follow.

What You Need

2 plants

water

box

paper and crayons

Sunlight and Leaves

Steps

1. Water both plants. Put them in a sunny place.

2. **Experiment** Draw a picture of each plant. Cover one plant with a box.

3. **Compare** Look at the plants after one week. Draw how each plant looks now.

STEP 1

STEP 2

STEP 3

Think and Share

1. **Infer** Compare your drawings with those of others. What differences do you find?

2. **Experiment** If your drawings are different, try the experiment again. Did the results change?

Guided Inquiry

Experiment What will happen to the covered plant if you leave the cover off? Predict and then try it.

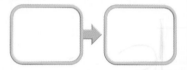

GPS **S1L1a.** Identify the basic needs of a plant. 1. Air; 2. Water; 3. Light; 4. Nutrients

Plants Need Sunlight

Plants need sunlight to live and grow. Plants use sunlight, air, and water to make their own food.

Express Lab

Activity Card 18
Model How Leaves Work

Which plant is not getting enough light?

All plants need light. Plants will not grow well if they do not get the light they need. Leaves that do not get enough light may turn yellow or brown.

▶ **Cause and Effect** What happens if a plant does not get enough light?

How Leaves Work

Most plants have leaves. The leaves take in sunlight and air to make food for the plant.

The food moves from the leaves to other parts of the plant. The plant uses the food to grow.

Different Kinds of Leaves

<u>Leaves come in many shapes and sizes.</u> Many leaves are flat. Some leaves have sharp points. Some trees have long, thin leaves called needles.

Pine trees have needles.

Holly leaves have sharp points.

▶ **Cause and Effect** What do leaves do for a plant?

oak leaf

Lesson Wrap-Up

❶ **Vocabulary** How do plants use **sunlight**?

❷ **Reading Skill** What might cause a plant's leaves to turn yellow or brown?

❸ **Predict** How can doing an experiment again help you check a prediction?

⌨ **Technology** Visit **www.eduplace.com/gascp** to find out more about plants.

LINKS
for Home and School

 STANDARDS S1CS2a. Use whole numbers in ordering, counting, identifying, measuring, and describing things and experiences. **M1N1b.** Correctly count and represent the number of objects in a set using numerals. **ELA1W1b.** Describes an experience in writing.

Math Count the Leaves

1. How many brown leaves are shown?

2. How many green leaves are shown?

3. Write a number sentence to show the total number of leaves.

 **Describe a Plant**

What parts do plants have? Write sentences that tell about plant parts. Draw a picture of your plant.

GeorgiaTask S1L1B

What are the parts of plants?

All plants have parts. Different plant parts do different things.

- Observe a plant.

- Draw a picture of the plant.

- Label the plant parts.

- Write what each part does.

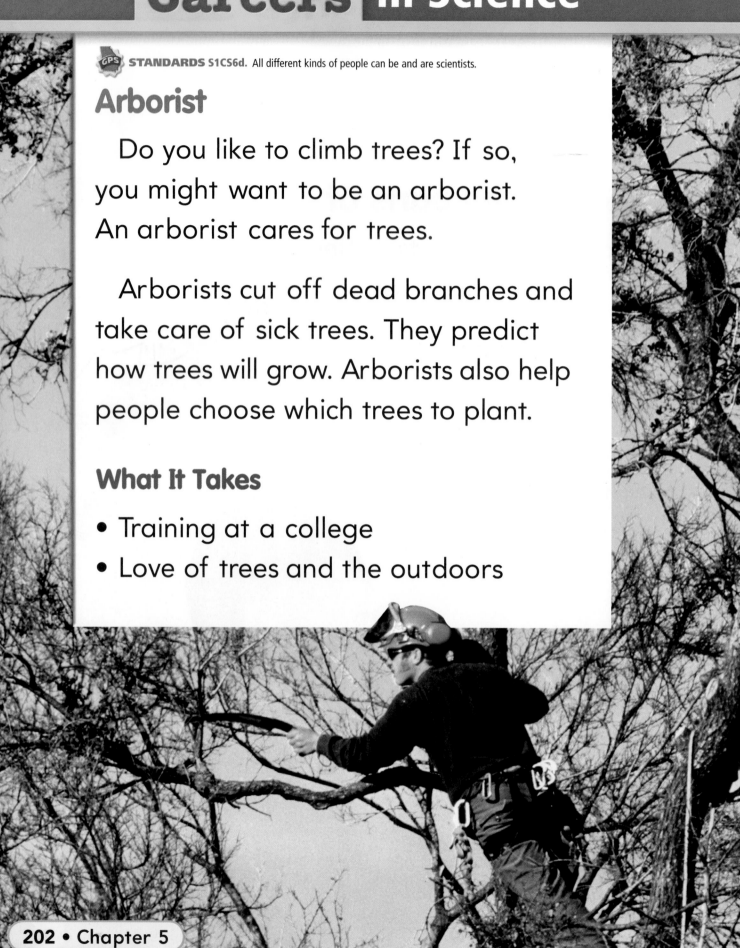

Careers in Science

STANDARDS S1CS6d. All different kinds of people can be and are scientists.

Arborist

Do you like to climb trees? If so, you might want to be an arborist. An arborist cares for trees.

Arborists cut off dead branches and take care of sick trees. They predict how trees will grow. Arborists also help people choose which trees to plant.

What It Takes

- Training at a college
- Love of trees and the outdoors

People in Science

STANDARDS S1CS6d. All different kinds of people can be and are scientists.

Ernesto Sandoval

Earth is home to many different plants. Collecting and growing plants is the job of Ernesto Sandoval. He works at a greenhouse. Mr. Sandoval makes sure plants get the air, water, light, and nutrients they need.

Visual Summary

Plants need sunlight, water, nutrients, air, and space. They have parts that help them meet their needs.

Plants need air, water, light, and space to live.	**Plants have parts that help them get what they need.**	**Roots take in water and nutrients from soil.**	**Leaves take in sunlight and air to make food.**

Main Ideas

1. What does a plant need to live? (p. 176)   S1L1a

2. How do roots help a plant? (pp. 188–189)   S1L1c

3. How do leaves help plants? (p. 198)   S1L1c

Vocabulary

Choose the correct word from the box.

S1CS7a

nutrients (p. 188)	
soil (p. 188)	
stem (p. 185)	

4. The part of a plant that connects the roots to other plant parts

5. The loose top layer of Earth

6. Materials in the soil that help plants grow

Using Science Skills

7. You and a friend get different results when you do a plant experiment. How can you find out who is right? S1CS6a

8. **Critical Thinking** How can people help plants that do not get what they need? S1L1a

 CRCT Prep

Choose a word to complete the sentence.

9. A _____ is the part of some plants that makes seeds.

    stem   flower   root

    Ⓐ   Ⓑ   Ⓒ   S1L1c

Chapter 6

Animals

Black bear

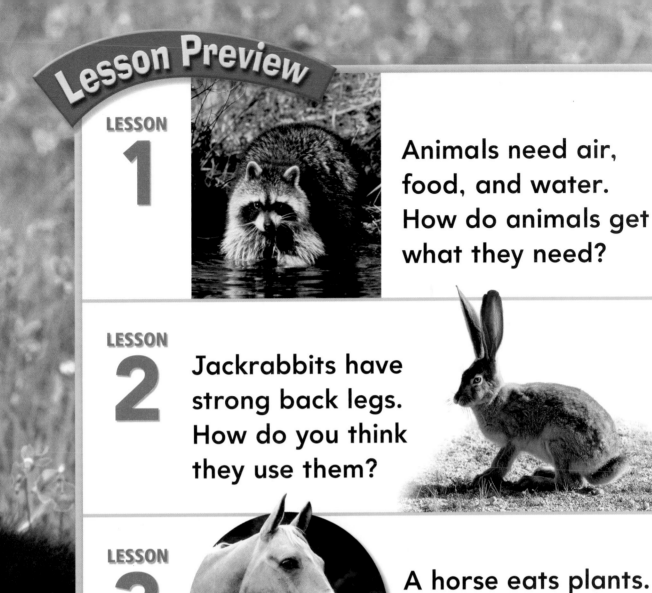

LESSON 1

Animals need air, food, and water. How do animals get what they need?

LESSON 2

Jackrabbits have strong back legs. How do you think they use them?

LESSON 3

A horse eats plants. What kind of teeth does a horse have?

Vocabulary

shelter p. 213

fins p. 224

wings p. 225

plant eater p. 230

meat eater p. 231

Picture Glossary p. H18

Vocabulary Skill

Use What's After

fins

wings

The ending **–s** has been added to these words. The ending means "more than one." Tell what each word means.

fins
Fins are body parts that fish use to move.

wings
Wings are body parts that birds use to fly.

meat eater

A meat eater is an animal that has sharp teeth to tear food.

shelter

A shelter is a safe place for animals to live.

Georgia
Performance Standards

Start with Your Standards

Habits of Mind

S1CS1a. Raise questions about the world around them and be willing to seek answers to some of the questions by making careful observations and measurements and trying to figure things out.

The Nature of Science

S1CS7d. Much can be learned about plants and animals by observing them closely, but care must be taken to know the needs of living things and how to provide for them. Advantage must be taken of classroom pets.

Life Science

S1L1b. Identify the basic needs of an animal.
1. air
2. water
3. food
4. shelter

S1L1d. Compare and describe various animals—appearance, motion, growth, basic needs.

GPS GEORGIA STANDARDS

S1CS7d. Much can be learned about plants and animals by observing them closely, but care must be taken to know the needs of living things and how to provide for them. Advantage must be taken of classroom pets.
S1L1b. Identify the basic needs of an animal.
1. air; 2. water; 3. food; 4. shelter

Essential Question
What Are the Needs of Animals?

Science and You

Animals need food, air, and water to live. They find those things where they live.

Inquiry Skill

Work Together Share what you observe with a partner.

What You Need

hermit crab in its home

hermit crab food

water

An Animal's Needs

Steps

1 Put the hermit crab home in a safe place. Give the hermit crab water and food.

STEP 1

2 **Work Together** Watch what the hermit crab does. Use words such as **above** and **next to** to tell where it goes.

STEP 2

3 **Record Data** Draw pictures. Show how the hermit crab gets what it needs to live.

STEP 3

Think and Share

1. **Work Together** Talk with your partner. How does a hermit crab use its home?

2. **Infer** What do animals need to live?

Guided Inquiry

Ask Questions Finish this question. How much food and water does a _____ need? Work together to find the answers.

▶ **Vocabulary**

shelter

▶ **Reading Skill**

Draw
Conclusions

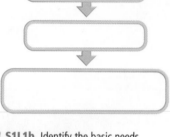

GPS S1L1b. Identify the basic needs
of an animal.
1. air
2. water
3. food
4. shelter

Animals Need Food

Animals need food, air, and water. Animals eat food when they are hungry. Plants and other animals are food for animals. Big animals need more food than small animals.

These cows are eating plants.

An eagle needs a larger
shelter than a hummingbird.

Shelter

Some animals need a shelter.
A **shelter** is a safe place for
animals to live. Some animals find
shelter in plants or other animals.
Many animals build shelters such
as nests. Some animals, such as
whales, do not use shelters at all.

▶ **Draw Conclusions**
How are the needs of big
and small animals alike?

Express Lab

Activity Card 19
Investigate Shelters

213

Animals Need Air and Water

All animals need air and water to live. Animals have body parts to help them get air. Many animals use their nose to breathe in air. Fish need air, too. They have gills to take in air from water.

gill

A tiger has a nose for breathing.

Whales come to the top of water to get air.

How is this mule deer getting what it needs?

Most animals get water by drinking. Some animals get water from the food they eat.

▶ **Draw Conclusions** What would happen if an animal did not get air and water?

Lesson Wrap-Up

❶ **Vocabulary** How does an animal use a **shelter**?

❷ **Reading Skill** How are all animals alike?

❸ **Work Together** How can sharing ideas help you learn more about animals?

🖥 **Technology** Visit **www.eduplace.com/gascp** to find out more about the needs of animals.

215

Animal Needs

How do different animals meet their needs? Five animal friends are about to find out!

Cast

Robin
Deer
Frog
Fish
Turtle

Deer: Hello, Robin. Hello, Frog. What are you doing here?

Frog: I am looking for food. I like to catch insects with my long tongue.

Robin: I'm here to find food for my babies. They like to eat worms.

Deer: I drink water from the lake. I eat leaves off bushes and trees.

Robin: I built my nest with twigs from bushes. My babies are safe in the nest now.

Frog: Oh dear! I'm not safe! I see a hawk in the sky. I have to go.

Deer: Frog, why don't you hide under the water? Frog?

Turtle: Frog has hopped away. But I can answer your question.

Deer: Please do!

Turtle: Frog cannot breathe under water. So he finds shelter behind a rock.

Fish: I can breathe under water. I can find shelter in the water, too.

Turtle: I take my shelter with me! I can tuck my head and legs into my shell.

Deer: Wow! We're lucky. We all can find everything we need right here where we live!

Sharing Ideas

1. **Write About It** Choose an animal. Write about how it meets its needs.

2. **Talk About It** Give hints about how an animal meets its needs. Have classmates guess the animal.

Lesson 2

GEORGIA STANDARDS

S1CS5a. Describe and compare things in terms of number, shape, texture, size, weight, color, and motion.
S1L1d. Compare and describe various animals—appearance, motion, growth, basic needs.

What Are the Parts of Animals?

Science and You

Body parts help animals get what they need to live.

Inquiry Skill

Classify Group living things that are alike in some way.

What You Need

animal pictures

crayons and paper

Animal Parts

Steps

1. **Compare** Look at the pictures. Tell how the animals are alike and different.

2. **Classify** Sort the animal pictures into groups that are alike in one way.

3. **Record Data** Name your groups. Draw pictures or write names to show the animals in each group.

Think and Share

1. **Classify** How did you group the animals?

2. **Infer** How might an animal use its long neck?

STEP 1

STEP 2

STEP 3

Guided Inquiry

Ask Questions Think of questions about how animals use body parts. Make a plan to find answers. Communicate what you find.

Habits of Mind

Vocabulary

fins

wings

Reading Skill

Main Idea and Details

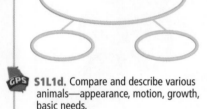

GPS **S1L1d.** Compare and describe various animals—appearance, motion, growth, basic needs.

Animal Body Parts

Animals use their body parts to find food and to stay safe. Animals use their eyes, ears, noses, legs, tails, and other parts to help them live.

Bush Baby

Large eyes help it see at night.

Ears help it find insects to eat.

Gray fur helps it hide in trees.

Legs and fingers help it catch food and hold on to trees.

Using Body Parts to Stay Safe

quills

stinger

claws

smell

sound

color and shape

Some animals can use body parts to hurt other animals or scare them away. Some animals have colors or shapes that help them hide.

▶ **Main Idea** What body parts help animals find food?

Express Lab

Activity Card 20
Model Feathers

223

Parts for Moving

Animals have body parts that they use to move. Animals move to find food. They move to get away from enemies.

A fish uses its tail and **fins** to move in water. A lion uses its strong legs to run and climb.

tail

fin

leg

wing

A bird uses its **wings** to fly through the air. A bird also uses its legs to walk, hop, and hold on to trees.

▶ **Main Idea** How does a bird use its legs?

Lesson Wrap-Up

❶ **Vocabulary** How does a fish use **fins** to live in water?

❷ **Reading Skill** Why do many animals have legs?

❸ **Classify** What kinds of body parts help animals stay safe?

🖥 **Technology** Visit **www.eduplace.com/gascp** to find out more about animal body parts.

EXTREME Science

Super Tongue

What *is* this bushy beast? It is not make-believe! Meet the giant anteater of Central America and South America.

The giant anteater is as long as a door is tall. It looks odd, but its body parts are perfect for an anteater!

The anteater's tongue is as long as your arm! It is rough and sticky. That helps it catch ants.

226 • Chapter 6

▼ **Snout** Its snout is long, but its mouth is very small.

A giant anteater uses powerful claws to dig up ants. It eats thousands of ants each day.

GPS GEORGIA STANDARDS

S1CS4a. Use a model—such as a toy or a picture—to describe a feature of the primary thing.
S1L1d. Compare and describe various animals—appearance, motion, growth, basic needs.

Essential Question

How Do Animals Use Their Mouths?

Science and You

Some animals have sharp teeth. Others have flat teeth. You can tell what an animal eats by looking at its teeth.

Inquiry Skill

Use Models Use something like a real thing to learn how the real thing works.

What You Need

human teeth model

pictures of animal teeth

paper and crayons

Sharp or Flat

Steps

① **Use Models** Observe the shapes of the model teeth.

STEP 1

② Think about the kinds of food you eat. Record how you use your different teeth.

STEP 2

③ **Compare** Look at the animal pictures. Decide which human teeth are like the teeth of each animal.

STEP 3

Think and Share

1. **Compare** What tooth shape would be helpful for tearing?

2. **Infer** How might the shape of an animal's teeth affect the kind of food it eats?

Guided Inquiry

Ask Questions Think about questions you have about the kinds of teeth different animals have. Work together to make a plan to find answers.

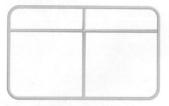
▶ **Vocabulary**

plant eater

meat eater

▶ **Reading Skill**

Compare and
Contrast

GPS **S1L1d.** Compare and describe various
animals—appearance, motion,
growth, basic needs.

Flat Teeth or Sharp Teeth

You can group animals
by what they eat. A **plant
eater** eats mostly plants.
That kind of animal has
flat teeth. A plant eater
uses its teeth to grind plants.

Zebras are plant eaters.

A lion is a meat eater.

A **meat eater** eats other animals. Meat eaters have sharp teeth. Their teeth help them tear meat.

Some animals have both flat teeth and sharp teeth. These animals eat both plants and animals.

▶ **Compare and Contrast** How are a lion's teeth different from a zebra's teeth?

Express Lab

Activity Card 21
Observe Teeth

Other Mouth Parts

Not all animals have teeth. <u>Some animals have different mouth parts to help them eat.</u>

A housefly has a mouth part that takes in water like a sponge.

A chameleon uses its long tongue to catch food.

Birds have beaks. A long beak helps a bird drink from a flower. Sharp beaks help birds crack open seeds.

A pelican has a large beak for catching fish.

▶ **Compare and Contrast** How is a pelican's mouth different from a chameleon's mouth?

Favoret page!

Lesson Wrap-Up

❶ **Vocabulary** What kind of teeth does a **plant eater** have?

❷ **Reading Skill** How are a plant eater's teeth different from a meat eater's teeth?

❸ **Use Models** How can a model of teeth help you understand what animals eat?

📷 **Technology** Visit **www.eduplace.com/gascp** to find out more about animal mouth parts.

233

LINKS
for Home and School

 STANDARDS S1CS2b. Readily give the sums and differences of single-digit numbers in ordinary, practical contexts and judge the reasonableness of the answer. **M1D1a.** Interpret tally marks, picture graphs, and bar graphs. **ELA1W1b.** Describes an experience in writing. **GeorgiaTask S1L1D**

Math Picture Graph

Look at the chart of children's pets that have four legs.

Mr. Williams's Class	
Pet with Four Legs	Number of Pets
cat	IIII
dog	III
hamster	I
turtle	II

Use the data to make a picture graph. Are there more cats or dogs?

 **Write a Story**

Write a story about how to take care of a pet. Draw pictures for your story. Tell how the pet gets what it needs to stay alive.

 STANDARDS S1L1d. Compare and describe various animals—appearance, motion, growth, basic needs.

How are animals different?

Compare two animals. How do they each find what they need to live?

- Find out how each animal moves. How does it get food and water?

- Find out where they live.

- Make a book about each animal. Add pictures.

STANDARDS S1CS6d. All different kinds of people can be and are scientists.

Zookeeper

Do you like animals? Maybe you would like to be a zookeeper!

Zookeepers care for animals at a zoo. They give them food, water, and baths. They make sure that animals have shelter.

What It Takes

- A love of animals
- For many jobs, four years of college

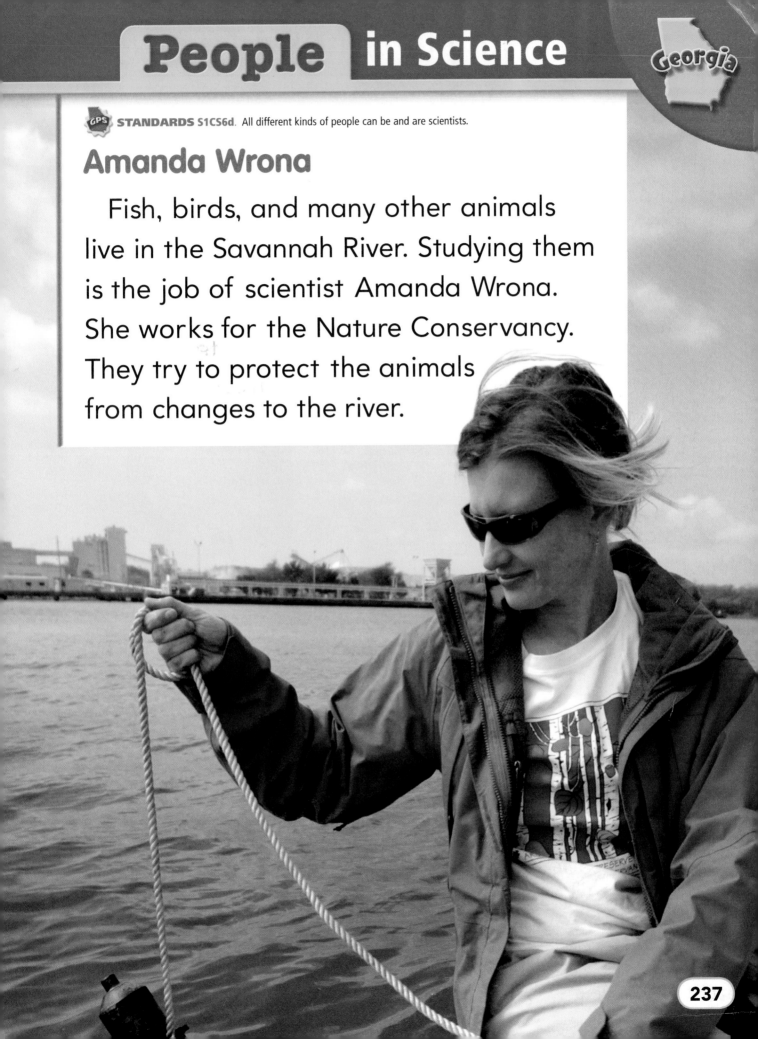

GPS STANDARDS **S1CS6d**. All different kinds of people can be and are scientists.

Amanda Wrona

Fish, birds, and many other animals live in the Savannah River. Studying them is the job of scientist Amanda Wrona. She works for the Nature Conservancy. They try to protect the animals from changes to the river.

Visual Summary

Animals have body parts that help them get what they need.

Animals need air, food, and water.	
Animals have parts for moving, breathing, and staying safe.	
Animals have different kinds of teeth for eating plants and meat.	

Main Ideas

1. What do animals need to live? **(p. 212)** `S1L1b`

2. How does a bush baby use its body parts? **(p. 222)** `S1L1d`

3. Where do animals find shelter? **(p. 213)** `S1L1b`

Vocabulary

Choose the correct word from the box.

S1CS7a

4. Parts of a bird that it uses to fly through the air

5. A safe place for animals to live

6. Parts of a fish that help it move

7. An animal that eats mostly plants

fins (p. 224)
plant eater (p. 230)
shelter (p. 213)
wings (p. 225)

Using Science Skills

8. Draw a picture of a meat eater's teeth. Then draw a picture of a plant eater's teeth. Label the pictures.   S1L1d

9. **Critical Thinking** Why isn't a bicycle an animal?   S1L1d

GPS CRCT Prep

10. What body parts do fish use to breathe?

   lungs   gills   nose
   Ⓐ   Ⓑ   Ⓒ   S1L1d

GPS Test Practice

Choose the correct answer.

1. Which animal needs more food?

   a dog   a mouse   a cow
   (A)   (B)   (C)   S1L1d

2. Plants and animals both need ___water___ to live.

   water   soil   shelter
                       (B)   (C)   S1L1a
                                                                   S1L1b

3. A plant's leaves turn yellow if it does not
   get enough

   soil.   flowers.   sunlight.
   (A)   (C)   S1L1a

4. Which picture shows an animal that only
   eats plants?

                                                     S1L1d

5. A plant's <u>roots</u> take in water and nutrients from the soil.

            flowers   roots   stems

             Ⓐ   Ⓑ   Ⓒ   `S1L1c`

6. Some animals need shelters to

            stay safe.   find food.   make food.

             Ⓐ   Ⓑ   Ⓒ   `S1L1b`

GPS Checking Main Ideas

Write the correct answer.

7. What can you tell about animals that have both flat teeth and sharp teeth?   `S1L1d`

8. What needs are being met for these baby birds?   `S1L1b`

You Can...

Discover More

What bird flaps its wings the fastest?

A hummingbird flaps its wings about 75 times every second! The wings move so fast that they make a humming sound. Hummingbirds are called nature's helicopters because of the way they move.

 Go to **www.eduplace.com/gascp** to learn more about the parts of a hummingbird.

Science and Math Toolbox

Using a Hand Lens

A hand lens is a tool that makes objects look bigger. It helps you see the small parts of an object.

Look at a Coin

1 Place a coin on your desk.

STEP 1

2 Hold the hand lens above the coin. Look through the lens. Slowly move the lens away from the coin. What do you see?

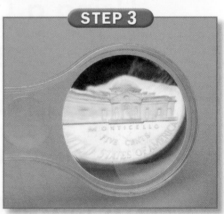

STEP 3

3 Keep moving the lens away until the coin looks blurry.

4 Then slowly move the lens closer. Stop when the coin does not look blurry.

STEP 4

Using a Thermometer

A thermometer is a tool used to measure temperature. Temperature tells how hot or cold something is. It is measured in degrees.

Find the Temperature of Water

1 Put water into a cup.

2 Put a thermometer into the cup.

3 Watch the colored liquid in the thermometer. What do you see?

4 Find the top of the red liquid. What number is next to it? That is the temperature of the water.

Using a Ruler

A ruler is a tool used to measure the length of objects. Rulers measure length in inches or centimeters.

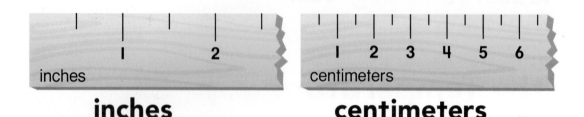

inches   **centimeters**

Measure a Crayon

1 Place the ruler on your desk.

2 Lay your crayon next to the ruler. Line up one end with the end of the ruler.

3 Look at the other end of the crayon. Which number is closest to that end?

Using a Calculator

A calculator is a tool that can help you add and subtract numbers.

Subtract Numbers

1 Tim and Anna grew plants. Tim grew 5 plants. Anna grew 8 plants.

2 How many more plants did Anna grow? Use your calculator to find out.

3 Enter **8** on the calculator. Then press the **–** key. Enter **5** and press **=** .

What is your answer?

Tim's Plants

Anna's Plants

Using a Balance

A balance is a tool used to measure mass. Mass is the amount of matter in an object.

Compare the Mass of Objects

1. Check that the pointer is on the middle mark of the balance. If needed, move the slider on the back to the left or right.

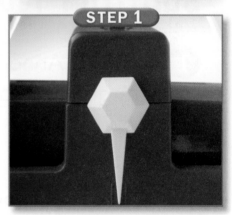

2. Place a clay ball in one pan. Place a crayon in the other pan.

3. Observe the positions of the two pans.

Does the clay ball or the crayon have more mass?

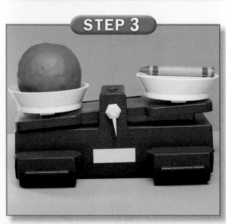

Making a Chart

A chart can help you sort information, or data. When you sort data it is easier to read and compare.

Make a Chart to Compare Animals

① Give the chart a title.

② Name the groups that tell about the data you collect. Label the columns with the names.

③ Carefully fill in the data in each column.

Which animal can move in the most ways?

How Animals Move

Animal	How It Moves
fish	swim
dog	walk, swim
duck	walk, fly, swim

Making a Tally Chart

A tally chart helps you keep track of items as you count.

Make a Tally Chart of Kinds of Pets

Jan's class made a tally chart to record the number of each kind of pet they own.

1. Every time they counted one pet, they made one tally.

2. When they got to five, they made the fifth tally a line across the other four.

3. Count the tallies to find each total.

How many of each kind of pet do the children have?

Kinds of Pets

🐱	cat	⅏⅏ ‖
🐶	dog	⅏⅏ ‖‖
🐹	hamster	‖‖

Making a Bar Graph

A bar graph can help you sort and compare data.

Make a Bar Graph of Favorite Pets

You can use the data in the tally chart on page H8 to make a bar graph.

1 Choose a title for your graph.

2 Write numbers along the side.

3 Write pet names along the bottom.

4 Start at the bottom of each column. Fill in one box for each tally.

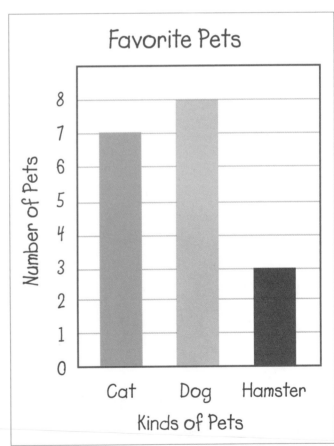

Which pet is the favorite?

Health and Fitness Handbook

Are you healthy? You are if you:

- know how your body works.
- practice safe actions when you play.
- know how to stay well.
- are active every day.
- eat healthful foods.

Inside Your Body

Your body has many parts. All the parts work together.

Brain

Your brain helps you think. It controls all your other body parts.

Lungs

Air goes in and out of your lungs. Your body needs air to stay alive.

Heart

Your heart pumps blood through your body. Your heart is about the size of your fist.

Stomach

Your stomach helps change food so your body can use it.

Bones and muscles hold you up and help you move.

Bones

Your body has more than 200 bones. Some bones protect body parts.

- Your skull protects your brain.
- Your ribs protect your heart and lungs.
- There are 27 bones in each of your hands.

Muscles

Muscles move body parts.

- The muscles in your legs are large. They help you run, jump, and play.
- The muscles in your eyelids are tiny. They help you blink.
- Your heart is a muscle, too.

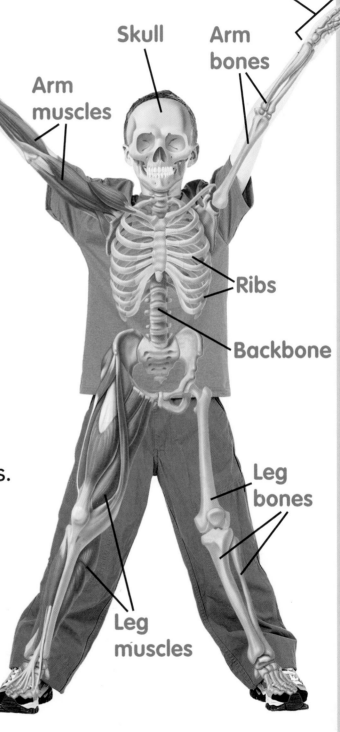

Hand bones

Skull

Arm bones

Arm muscles

Ribs

Backbone

Leg bones

Leg muscles

Foods for Healthy Bones and Teeth

Your body needs calcium. Calcium makes bones and teeth strong. Get the right amount of calcium by eating three of these foods every day!

Dairy Foods

- milk
- yogurt
- cheese

Foods With Calcium Added

- cereal bars
- wheat bread
- cereal
- juices
- tofu
- waffles

Other Foods

- spinach
- bok choy
- garbanzo beans
- almonds

These foods give you one serving of calcium.

calcium-added orange juice

breakfast bar

two burritos

macaroni and cheese

Caring for Your Teeth

You use your teeth to chew, talk, and smile.

Brush Twice Each Day

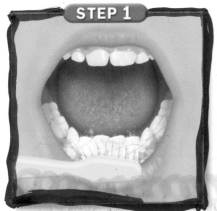

STEP 1

Brush the fronts.

STEP 2

Brush the backs.

STEP 3

Brush the tops.

Floss Once Each Day

STEP 1

Wrap the floss and pull it tight.

STEP 2

Slide the floss between teeth.

Dental Check-Ups

Dentists and dental hygienists clean and check your teeth. They use x-ray machines to check the hidden parts of teeth.

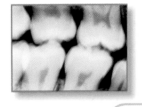

Fun and Fit on the Playground

Have Some Fun

It's time to go outside. How will you play today? Being active keeps your body fit. You feel good when you are fit. You can play hard and not get tired. You can bend your body in many ways.

Throw, kick, and catch.

Getting and Staying Fit

Do different activities to get fit and stay fit. Stretch before you start. Play hard. Then stretch again. Try these Fun and Fit ideas.

Climb, skip, or swing.

Have fun with friends.

A Safe Bike

You probably know how to ride a bike. Is your bike the right size? Your feet should reach the pedals easily. Your body should be above the bar when you stand.

Safety Equipment

Wear a helmet every time you ride. It should fit flat and protect your forehead. Pull the strap tight.

The right equipment can help keep you safe.

bell

front reflector

rear reflector

reflector

pedal reflectors

Picture Glossary

A

attract

When objects pull toward each other. A magnet attracts iron and steel. (134)

C

classify

Sort objects into groups that are alike in some way.

cloud

Many drops of water together. (31)

communicate

Share what you learn with others by talking, drawing pictures, or making charts and graphs.

compare
Look for ways that objects or events are alike or different.

experiment

Make a plan to collect data and then share the results with others.

fall
The season that follows summer. In fall, the weather gets cooler. (44)

fins
Body parts that help a fish move. (224)

flower
The part of a plant that makes seeds. (185)

H19

freeze

To change from a liquid to a solid.
A pond may freeze in winter. (61)

hail

Round ice and hard snow that
falls during thunderstorms. (70)

heat

Heat makes things warm. (96)

infer

Use what you observe and know
to tell what you think.

leaves

Parts of a plant that make food
for the plant. (185)

light
You can see light. (106)

magnet

An object that pulls iron and steel toward it. (134)

magnetic

An object that is attracted by a magnet. (134)

magnetic field
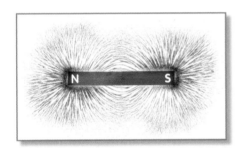
The space around a magnet where the magnet's force works. (142)

magnetic force

The pushing or pulling force of a magnet. (148)

measure

Use different tools to collect data about the properties of objects.

meat eater

An animal that eats other animals. A meat eater has sharp teeth. (231)

melt

To change from a solid to a liquid. Ice on a frozen pond will melt in spring. (62)

nutrients

Materials in soil that plants need to grow. (188)

observe

Use tools and the senses to learn about the properties of an object or event.

pitch

How high or low a sound is.
A violin has a high pitch. (120)

plant eater

An animal that eats mostly plants.
A plant eater has flat teeth. (230)

poles

The places on a magnet where
the forces are strongest. (136)

predict

Use what you know and patterns
you observe to tell what will
happen.

rain

Water that falls in drops from
clouds. (60)

record data
Write or draw to show what you have observed.

repels
When a magnet pushes an object away from itself. Like poles of magnets repel each other. (137)

roots
The parts of a plant that take in water from the ground. (185)

S

season
A time of year that has its own kind of weather. (36)

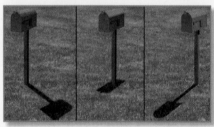

shadow
Something that forms when an object blocks light. (109)

shelter
A safe place for animals to live.
(213)

sleet
Water that falls as frozen or
partly frozen raindrops. (69)

snow
Ice that falls from clouds. (68)

soil
The loose top layer of Earth.
(188)

sound
You can hear sound. Birds make
sounds when they sing. (114)

spring
The season that follows winter.
Many baby animals are born
in spring. (36)

stem

Part of a plant that connects the roots to the other plant parts. (185)

summer

The season that follows spring. Summer is the warmest season. (38)

sunlight

Light from the Sun. (176)

T

temperature

How warm or cool something is. The temperature is cold when there is snow. (22)

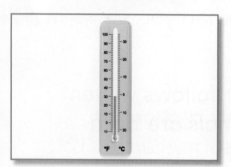

thermometer

A tool that measures temperature. (22)

use data

Measurements of My Plants	
Date	Measurement
October 1	3 inches
November 1	4 inches
December 1	$4\frac{1}{2}$ inches
January 1	5 inches

Use what you observe and record to find patterns and make predictions.

use models

Use something like the real thing to understand how the real thing works.

use numbers

Count, measure, order, or estimate to describe and compare objects and events.

vibrates

Moves back and forth very fast. A drum vibrates when you strike it. (114)

volume

How loud or soft a sound is. A whisper has soft volume. (121)

water cycle
Water moving from Earth to the sky and back again. (30)

weather
What the air outside is like. (16)

wings
Body parts that help a bird fly through the air. (225)

winter
The season that follows fall. Winter is the coldest season. (46)

work together
Work as a group to share ideas, data, and observations.

A

Air
- for animals, 212, 214–215
- movement of, 99
- for plants, 176, 196, 198–199

Animals
- caring for, 236
- colors of, 223
- differences in, 234–235
- food for, 167, 212, 227, 230–233
- in Georgia, 164–167
- growth of, 39, 166–167
- hearing of, 110–111
- homes of, 164–167, 209, 213
- meat eaters, 164–167, 209, 231
- mouths of, 226–233
- movement of, 224–225
- needs of, 164–167, 209–219
- observing, 168–169
- parts of, 208, 214, 220–233
- plant eaters, 230
- protection for, 223–225
- seasons and, 37, 39–41, 45, 47
- shape of, 223
- shelter for, 164–167, 209, 213
- survival of, 164–167, 222–225
- teeth of, 228–231
- types of, 164–167, 208–209, 214–215, 223, 230–231
- vocabulary on, 212, 222, 230
- water for, 212, 214–215

Anteaters, 226–227
Arborist, 202

B

Balance scale, 59, H6
Bats, 110–111
Beaks, 233
Bentley, Wilson, 72–73
Bike safety, H17
Birds, 208, 213, 225, 233, 242
Bobcats, 164, 166–167
Bones, H13
Brain, H12
Bush baby, 222

C

Calcium, H14
Calculators, H5
Cars, S11
Caterpillar, 37
Chameleon, 232
Charts, 21, 59, 67, 74, 95, 133, 152, H7–H8
Cirrus clouds, 32
Clouds
- comparing, 31–33
- precipitation from, 28, 68–71
- rain and, 28, 60
- types of, 32–33
- water drops in, 31

Cocoon, 37
Coils, 139
Coins, H2
Computer scientist, 154
Cows, 212
Cumulus clouds, 33

D

Dairy foods, H14
Davis, Betty, 49

Decision-making, S14–S15
Deer, 215
Dental care, H15
Dermody, Neil, S10
Directed Inquiry, 14, 20, 28, 34, 42, 58, 66, 94, 104, 112, 118, 132, 140, 146, 174, 182, 186, 194, 210, 220, 228
Drums, 116

E

Eagles, 213
Exercise, H16

F

Fall, 42–45
Fins, 208, 224
Fire
- heat from, 97, 99
- light from, 106

Firefly, 107
Fireworks, 107
Fish, S4–S5, 208, 224
Floods, 64
Flowers, 184–185
Food
- for animals, 212, 227, 230–233
- for humans, H14
- for plants, 198–199

Freeze, 56, 61
Friction, 97
Fruits, 39

Index

 G

Geese, 37, 45
Georgia
  animals in, 164–167
  aquarium, 161
  sounds in, 84–87
  temperatures in, 5–7
  weather in, 4–7
  winter in, 6–7
Georgia standards,
  S1–S6
Gills, 214
Goldfish, S4–S5
Graphs,
  bar, 50, 175, H9
  picture, 234
Greenhouse, 203

 H

Hail, 56, 70–71
Hand lens, H2
Hands-On Projects, 8–9,
  88–89, 168–169
Health and Fitness,
  H10–H17
Healthy foods, H14
Heart, H12
Heat
  changes from, 98–103
  for cooking, 93, 98,
    100–103
  from fire, 97, 99
  from friction, 97
  measuring, 94–95
  moving things, 99
  from Sun, 96, 98
  vocabulary on, 96
House, Donna, S2–S3
Housefly, 232
Hummingbirds, 213, 242
Hybrid cars, S11

 I

Ice
  in cold weather, 68–69
  freezing, 61
  melting, 62, 98
  in warm weather, 70–71
Inquiry Skills
  ask questions, 29,
    104–105, 141, 183,
    211, 221, 229
  be an inventor, 21, 119
  classify, 42–43, 105,
    220–221
  communicate, 34–35,
    43, 67
  compare, 28–29, 43,
    59, 67, 95, 113, 133,
    175, 182–183, 195,
    221, 229
  experiment, 35, 95,
    133, 147, 175, 187,
    194–195
  infer, 29, 35, 67, 95,
    113, 119, 140–141,
    147, 175, 186–187,
    195, 211, 221, 229
  measure, 20–21, 29,
    58–59, 67, 94–95,
    174–175
  observe, 15, 29, 66–67,
    105, 112–113, 119,
    132–133, 141, 183
  predict, 29, 35, 59, 105,
    146–147
  record data, 14–15, 21,
    59, 95, 105, 113, 119,
    133, 141, 175, 183,
    187, 211, 221
  solve a problem, 43,
    113
  use data, 118, 119
  use models, 228–229
  use numbers, 59
  work together, 15,
    210–211
Instruments, 88–89, 115,
  116, 120

Inventor, S10–S13
Investigations, *See*
  Directed Inquiry.
Iron filings, 140–142

 K

Kammen, Bamidele, 155

 L

Lamb, 39
Leaves
  changes in, 44
  of plants, 172, 184–185
  purpose of, 184–185,
    194–195, 198–199
  sunlight and, 194–199
  types of, 192–193, 199
Light. *See also* Sunlight
  for plants, 176, 181, 197
  shadows and, 108–109
  shining, 104–105
  from Sun, 92, 96, 106
  vocabulary on, 106
Light bulbs, 97, 107
Lighthouse, 104
Lily pads, 192–193
Lions, 224, 231
Liquids, 60–61
Literature
  "City Rain," 27
  Rain, 26
Lizards, 40
Luna moth, 37
Lungs, H12

 M

Maglev Trains, 138–139
Magnetic coils, 139
Magnetic fields, 130,
  140–142, 150

Index

Index

Credits

Permission Acknowledgements

Excerpt from *Something New Begins* by Lilian Moore. Copyright © 1967, 1982 by Lilian Moore. Used by permission of Marian Reiner. *Rain* by Manya Stojic. Copyright © 2000 by Manya Stojic. Used by permission of Crown Publishers, Inc., a division of Random House Inc. *City Rain* by Rachel Field. Copyright © 1926 by Doubleday, a division of Random House, Inc. from *Taxis and Toadstools* by Rachel Field. Used by permission of Random House Children's Books, a division of Random House, Inc. *The Dragonfly* by Eleanor Farjeon. Copyright © 1933, 1961 by Eleanor Farjeon. Reprinted by permission of Harold Ober Associates Incorporated.

Cover and Title Page

Front cover (sea otter) © Kevin Schafer/CORBIS. (kelp) © Gerry Ellis/Minden Pictures. (starfish) © Tom and Pat Leeson Photography. (water background) © David Fleetham/Alamy. Back cover © Peter Essick/Aurora/Getty Images. Spine © Kevin Schafer/CORBIS. Title page © Kevin Schafer/CORBIS. End Paper End Paper (t) Lightwave Photography, Inc./Animals Animals. (b) © Jeff Foot/Dcom/DRK Photo.

Photography

v ©Gabriel Eckert. vi ©Kevin Barry. viii Richard Levine/Alamy Images. ix W. Perry Conway/Corbis. S2 William A. Bake/Corbis. S6 © Wesley Hitt/Mira.com. UAUO ©NTPL/Ian Shaw/The Image Works. UA01–2 Image Source/PictureQuest. 2–3 Image Source/Alamy Images. 4–7 ©Gabriel Eckert. (l) ©J.Greenberg/PhotriMicroStock. (inset) John Bazemore/AP Photo. 9 Royalty Free/Corbis. 10–11 (bkgrd) Alan Schein Photography/Corbis. (tr) ©Vincent Hobbs/SuperStock. (cr) Royalty Free/Corbis. (bl) Chinch Gryniewicz; Ecoscene/Corbis. (br) Royalty-Free/Corbis. 12–13 (bkgrd) ©Tom Bean/DRK Photo. (t)Ariel Skelley/Corbis. (bl) ©David Carriere/Index Stock Images. (cl) ©George E. Jones 111/Photo Researchers, Inc. (cr) © E. R. Degginger/Color Pic, Inc. (br) ©Leonard Lee Ruell/Animals Animals-Earth Scenes. 14 (bkgrd) Stephen St John/National Geographic/Getty Images. (l) Ariel Skelley/Corbis. 16 (b) ©Michael Newman/Photo Edit, Inc. 17 (l) Douglas Peebles/Corbis. (br) Ariel Skelley/Corbis. 18 ©2001. Cynthia Malaran http://www.malaran.com from the website http://www.watchingthechanges.com All Rights Reserved. 19 Robert Glusic/Photodisc/Getty Images. 20–21 (bkgrd) ©Burgess Blevins. (b) Robert Holmes/Corbis. 22 Jeff Cadge/The Image Bank/Getty Images. 23 (bkgrd) Image Source/Alamy Images. (r) AJA Productions/The Image Bank/Getty Images. 24 (l) ©David Young-Wolff/Photo Edit, Inc. (r) ©Jeff Grennberg/Photo Edit, Inc. 25 (l) ©David Young-Wolff/Photo Edit, Inc. (r) ©Tony Freeman/Photo Edit, Inc. 28–29 (bkgrd) Craig Tuttle/Corbis. 30–31 ©Jim Steinberg/Photo Researchers, Inc. 32–33 (bkgrd) ©Terry Eggers/Panoramic Images. (t) ©Tom Bean/DRK Photo. (r) ©Brock May/Photo Researchers,Inc. 34–35

(bl) ©Kim Taylor and Jane Burton/DK Images. (bkgrd) Peter Adams Photography/Alamy Images. 36 (b) Peter Dean/Getty Images. 37 (l) ©Dwight Kuhn. (c) ©Bob Jensen/Bruce Coleman, Inc. (r) Dynamic Graphics Group/Creatas/Alamy Images. (t) Julie Habel/Corbis. 38 Ariel Skelley/Corbis. 39 (t) Ed Young/Corbis. (b) Premium Stock/Corbis. 42–43 (bkgrd) ©Julio Lopez Saguar/Photonica. (bl) Siede Preis/Photodisc/Getty Images. 44 (b) Ron Chapple/Thinkstock/Getty Images. 45 (c) ©Gabriel Eckert. (t) ©William H. Mullins/Photo Researchers, Inc. (b) ©Dwight Kuhn. 46 (r) Mike Powell/The Image Bank/Getty Images. (bl) ©Steve Skjold/Photo Edit, Inc. 47 ©Thomas Mangelsen/Minden Pictures. 48 (l) David Carriere/IndexStock. (t) ©George E. Jones 111/Photo Researchers, Inc. (r) ©Leonard Lee Ruell/Earth Scenes/Animals Animals. (b ©E.R Degginger/Color Pic, Inc. 49 ©Courtesy of Betty Davis. 51 D. Hurst/Alamy Images. (inset) ©John Howard/Photo Researchers, Inc. 54–55 (bkgrd) Richard Heinzen/SuperStock. (c) Ken Hawkins/Corbis SYGMA. (tr) Rainman/zefa/Corbis. 56 (bkgrd) ©Mary Altaffer/AP Photo. (t) ©David Young-Wolff/Photo Edit, Inc. 57 (t) A.T. Willett/Alamy Images. (b) ©Richard Hutchings/Photo Edit, Inc. 58–59 Royalty-Free/Corbis. 60 (tr) Poligons Photo Index/Alamy Images. (c) ©David Young-Wolff/Photo Edit, Inc. (bl) Anthony-Masterson/Getty Images. 61 ©Barbara Stitzer/Photo Edit, Inc. 63 Gay Bumgarner/IndexStock. 66 (bkgrd) William A. Bake/Corbis. (bl) © Perennou Nuridsany/Photo Researchers, Inc. 67 (inset) ©John Bazemore/AP Photo. (c) ©Gabriel Eckert. 68 (b) ©Richard Hutchings/Photo Edit, Inc. (inset) © Perennou Nuridsany/Photo Researchers, Inc. 69 (t) ©Dennis MacDonald/Photo Edit, Inc. 70 (inset) ©Jim Reed/Science Photo Library/Photo Researchers, Inc. (c) A.T. Willett/Alamy Images. 71 © Rogers Edwards. 72–73 ©Wilson Bentley Digital Archives of the Jericho Historical Society/snowflakebentley.com. 72 (br) © Perennou Nuridsany/Photo Researchers, Inc. (cr) ©Kenneth Libbrecht/Science Photo Library/Photo Researchers, Inc. 75 Gari Wyn Williams/Alamy Images. 76 (l) ©David Young-Wolff/Photo Edit, Inc. (cl) ©Richard Hutchings/Photo Edit, Inc. (cr) ©Mary Altaffer/AP photo. (r) A. T Willet/Alamy Images. 80 (r) ©Ed Jackson. (l) ©Patricia Masters. UBUO ©Graeme Teague Photography. UB01–83 ©David Young-Wolff/Photo Edit, Inc. 84 (bkgrd) William A. Bake/Corbis. (l) Jozsef Szasz-Fabian/Shutter Stock. (r) DLILLC/Corbis. 85 (inset) Geoff Campbell/ShutterStock. 86–87 (bkgrd) ©Graeme Teague Photography. (br) ©Graeme Teague Photography. (tl) ©Ron Sherman Photography. 90–91 (bkgrd) Jeff Hunter/The Image Bank/Getty Images. (tr) Stock Connection Blue/Alamy Images. (cl) Profimedia International s.r.o./Alamy Images. (br) Gavriel Jecan/Corbis. (b) Panoramic Images/Getty Images. 92 ©Kevin Barry. 93 (t) ©Daniel Barillot/Masterfile. (b) ©Michael Newman/Photo Edit, Inc. 94–95 Goodshot/Alamy Images. 96 Richard T. Nowitz/Corbis. 97 (t) Alchemy/Alamy Images. (c) Courtesty of Lennox Hearth Products. 98 (t) Reuters/Corbis. (b) ©Daniel Barillot/Masterfile. 102 Image Source/Picturequest/Jupiterimages. 104 (l) Stuart Westmorland/Stone/Getty Images. (bkgrd) ©Wei Yan/Masterfile. 106 ©Kevin Barry. 107 (tc) ©E. R. Degginger/

Color Pic, Inc. (b) ©Phil Degginger/Color Pic, Inc. 109 C Squared Studio/Photodisc/Getty Images. 113 (b) ©Michael & Patricia Fogden/Minden Pictures. (bkgrd) ©Gunter Ziesler/Peter Arnold Inc. 114 Nasa. 115 ©Gregory Scott/DK Images. 117 ©Michael Newman/Photo Edit, Inc. 118 (b) ©Michael Newman/Photo Edit, Inc. (bkgrd) ©Michael Newman/Photo Edit, Inc. 120 ©Steve Shott/DK Images. 121 (t) ©David Young-Wolff/Photo Edit, Inc. (b) ©Michael Newman/Photo Edit, Inc. 122 (t) Science Photos/Alamy Images. (c) ©Philip Rostron/Masterfile. 123 ©Michael Newman/Photo Edit, Inc. 126 (l) Harald Sund/The Image Bank/Getty Images. (c) Alchemy/Alamy Images. 129 Noeru Takizawa/Photonica/Getty Images. 130 ©Michael Newman/Photo Edit, Inc. 138–139 LIU Jin/AFP/Getty Images. 146 Tim Pannell/Corbis. 154 ©Michael Newman/Photo Edit, Inc. 155 (b) ©Gary Turchin/Chilldren's Hopital and Research Center, Oakland. (t) Lester Lefkowitz/Corbis. UCUO Courtesy of Georgia Aquarium. UCUO–161 Courtesy of Georgia Aquarium. 162–163 ©Joern Sackermann/Bilderberg/Peter Arnold, Inc. 164 ©ComStock/FotoSearch. 165 (t) ©Alvin E. Staffan/Photo Researchers, Inc. (b) ©Adam Jones/Photo Researchers, Inc. 166–167 (bkrgd) Andrew Darrington/Alamy Images (c) W. Perry Conway/Corbis. 170–171 (bkgrd) ©Art Wolfe, Inc. (t) Craig Lovell/Corbis. (tc) ©TH Foto-Stockfood Munich/Stockfood America. (r) ©Dwight Kuhn. (b) ©Walter Chandoha/Chandoha Photography. 172 (t) ©Geoff Bryant/Photo Researchers, Inc. (c) ©Phil Degginger/Color Pic, Inc. 173 (bkgrd) ©Ralph A. Clevenger/Corbis. (l) Jose Luis Pelaez, Inc./Corbis. 174–175 Paul Springett/Alamy Images. 176 Richard Levine/Alamy Images. 179 Michael Boys/Corbis. 180–181 (bkgrd) Royalty-Free/Corbis. (c) Lowell Georgia/Corbis. 182–183 (l) Miyoko Komine/Amana Images/Getty Images. (bkgrd) Carles Mauzy/Corbis. 184 ©Phil Degginger/Color Pic, Inc. 185 (t) Jack Tait/Alamy Images. (bc) ©Phil Degginger/Color Pic, Inc. (b) ©Phil Degginger/Color Pic, Inc. 186–187 (bkgrd) ©Kathy Atkinson/OSF/Animals Animals. (b) ©Kathy Atkinson/OSF/Animals Animals. 189 (tl) ©James Randklev/ChromoSohm Media Inc./Photo Researchers, Inc. (tr) ©Wayne Lawler/Photo Researchers, Inc. 190 (l) ©Dwight Kuhn. (br) ©Michael Fogden/DRK Photo. 191 ©Steve Gorton/DK Images. 194–195 (bkgrd) ©Greg Gawlowski/Dembinsky Photo Associates. (b) ©Maxine Cass. 196–197 (bkgrd) Michael Busselle/Taxi/Getty Images. (t) ©Breck Kent/EarthScenes/AnimalsAnimals. 199 (t) ©Scott Camazine/Medical, Science and Nature Images. (c) ©Matthew Ward/DK Images. (b) ©Animals Animals/Earth Scenes. 202 Skipp Nall/Getty Images. 203 Courtesy of Ernesto Sandoval. 204 (l) ©Fotopic/Omni-Photo communication. (c) ©Phil Degginger/Color Pic, Inc. (cr) ©Phil Degginger/Color Pic, Inc. (r) © blickwinkel/Alamy. 206–207 (bkgrd) ©Daniel J. Cox/Natural Exposures. (t) Chase Swift/Corbis. (c) Jonathan Blair/Corbis. (b) ©Lacz, Gerard/Animals Animals-Earth Scenes. 208–209 (bkgrd) ©Tomas & Pat Leeson/Photo Researchers, Inc. (t) Masa Ushioda/Stephen Frink Collection/Alamy Images. (b) Joe McDonald/Corbis. 209 ©Jerry Young/DK Images. 210–211 (bkgrd) ©Kunst & Scheidulin/Premium/Panoramic Images. (b) ©Robert Lubeck/

Animals Animals. **212** Liang Zhuoming/ Corbis. **213** (t) ©Bob & Clara Calhoun/ Bruce Coleman, Inc. (l) ©Jeff Foott/Bruce Coleman, Inc. **214** (l) Photolibrary.com/ Getty Images. (t) ©Morse. Randy/Animals Animals-Earth Scenes. (b) ©Tom Brakefield/ DRK Photo. **215** ©Carl R. Sams, II/ Dembinsky Photo Associates. **220–221** (bkgrd) ©Greg Dimijian/Photo Researchers, Inc. (l) ©Laura Riley/Bruce Coleman, Inc. **222** ©Dave King/DK Images. **223** (tl) ©Nigel Dennis/Photo Researchers, Inc. (tc) Bach/Zefa/Masterfile. (tr) ©Michael DeYoung/AlaskaStock. (bl) ©Tom Brake-field/Corbis. (bc) ©E.R. Degginger/Color Pic, Inc. (br) ©E.R. Degginger/Color Pic, Inc. **224** Masa Ushioda/Stephen Frink Collection/Alamy Images. **225** (l) ©Alan & Sandy Carey/Photo Researchers, Inc.(r) Joe McDonald/Corbis. **228–229** (bkgrd) Aaron Farley/Botanica/Jupterimages. (b) Lester Lefkowitz/Photographers Choice/Getty Images. **230** (b) Bobby Model/National Geographic/Getty Images. (l) Karl Ammann/Digital Vision/Getty Images. **231** (t) S Purdy Matthews/Stone/Getty Images. (b) Gallo Images-Roger De La Harpe/The Image Bank/Getty Images. **232** (t) F. Rauschenbach/Zefa/Corbis. (b) Bob Elsdale/The Image Bank/Getty Images. **233** ©SeaPics. **236** (b) Jim Naughten/Stone/ Getty Images. (bkgrd) Jim Naughten/ Stone/Getty Images. **237** Courtesy of Amanda Wrona. **238** (tl) ©Robert Lubeck/ Animals Animals. (tr) ©Carl R. Sams, II/ Dembinsky Photo Associates. (cl) ©Dave King/DK Images. (cr) ©Morse. Randy/ Animals Animals-Earth Scenes. (bl) Karl Ammann/Digital Vision/Getty Images. (br) Gallo Images-Roger De La Harpe/The Image Bank/Getty Images. **242** (l) ©Dominique Braud/Dembinsky Photo Associates, Inc. (r) ©Dominique Braud/ Dembinsky Photo Associates, Inc.

Assignment

© HMCo./Ken Karp Photography: **iv, vii, i, S5, 8, 9, 14–15, 20–21, 28, 29, 42, 43, 51, 58, 59, 62, 66** (r), **67, 82–83, 88–89, 93–94, 99–100, 101–103, 107, 116, 125–126, 128–131, 135–136, 140** (bl), **142, 146–151, 153, 156** (br), **168–169, 172, 174, 175, 177, 182, 183, 186, 187, 194, 195, 201, 211, 216–218, 221, 229, 235.**
© HMCo./Richard Hutchings Photography: **34, 35, 66** (b), **95, 105, 113, 119, 124, 130, 132–133, 134–135, 137, 140** (t), **141, 143, 156** (bl).
©HMCo./Lawrence Migdale Photography: **97, 108, 115.**

Illustration

UAUO Nick Diggory/Illustrationweb. **5** Nick Diggory. **11, 22, 23,** Promotion Studios. **66** Pamela Thomson. **74** Luvy Delgado. **UBUO** Nick Diggory/Illustrationweb.**100–103**

Cheryl Mendenhall. **139** Patrick Gnan. **160** David Klug. UC Opener Nick Diggory/ Illustrationweb. **178** Jeff Wack. **188** Phil Wilson. **197** Wendy Smith. **234** Daniel Del Valle.

Extreme Science

40–41 © Tim Davis/Corbis. **64–65** AP Photo/Stephen Morton. **65** (inset) © ExtremeInstability.com. **110–111** Terry Rishel/© Dale Chihuly. **111** (t) Mark Wexler/© Dale Chihuly Studio. **144–145** Patrick Walters/Coasterimage.com. **192–193** China Photos/Getty Images. **208** © Joe McDonald/Corbis. **226–227** © Frans Lanting/Minden Pictures. **227** (b) © Shawn Gould.

Nature of Science

PHOTOGRAPHY: (kangaroo) © Martin Rugner/age Fotostock. **S1** © Digital Vision. **S2–3** © Tim Sloan/AFP/Getty. **S3** (r) Photo courtesy of the National Museum of the American Indian, Smithsonian Institution. **S4–5** © HMCo./Joel Benjamin Photography. **S6–7** © HMCo./Ed Imaging. **S8–9** © HMCo./Ed Imaging. **S10** Julie Dermody. **S11** © Issei Kato/Reuters/Corbis. **S12** © HMCo./Joel Benjamin Photography. **S14** © HMCo./Joel Benjamin Photography. **S16** © HMCo./Richard Hutchings Photography.

Health and Fitness Handbook

ASSIGNMENT: **H12, H13,** © HMCo./ Coppola Studios Inc. **H15, H17** © HMCo./Joel Benjamin. ILLUSTRATION: **H12, H13,** Bart Vallecoccia. **H17** Linda Lee.

Science and Math Toolbox

H7 (t) John Giustina/Getty Images. (m) Georgette Douwma/Getty Images. (b) Giel/ Getty Images. **H8** Photodisc/Getty Images.

Picture Glossary

PHOTOGRAPHY: **H18** Royalty Free/Corbis. **H19** Ron Chapple/Thinkstock/Getty Images. (tb) Masa Ushioda/Stephen Frink Collection/Alamy Images. (b) Jack Tait/ Alamy Images. **H20** ©Stephen G. Maka/ DRK Photo. (tc) A.T. Willet/Alamy Images. (c) Courtesty of Lennox Hearth Products. (b) ©Scott Camazine. **H21** (t) Harald Sund/ The Image Bank/Getty Images. (c) ©HMco. **H22** (t) Gallo Images-Roger De La Harpe/ The Image Bank/Getty Images. (tc) ©Stephen G. Maka/DRK Photo. **H23** (t) ©Steve Shott/DK Images. (tc) Karl Ammann/Digital Vision/Getty Images. (b) ©David Young-Wolff/Photo Edit, Inc. **H24** (c) Steve Gorton/DK Images. (green leaves) David Carriere/Index Stock Imagery. (pink flowers) ©E.R Degginger/Color Pic, Inc.

(berries) ©Leonard Lee Ruell/Animals Animals -Earth Scenes. (fall leaves) ©George E. Jones 111/Photo Researchers, Inc. **H25** (fox) ©Tom & Pat Leeson/Photo Researchers, Inc. (umbrellas) ©Mary Altaffer/AP Photo. (snowman) ©Richard Hutchings/Photo Edit, Inc. (canary) ©Gregory Scott/DK Images. (ducks) Julie Habel/Corbis. **H26** (t) Rich Iwasaki/Stone/ Getty Images. (tc) Ariel Skelley/Corbis. (c) ©Mark Gibson Stock Photography. (tb) Jeff Cadge/The Image Bank/Getty Images. **H27** ©Michael Newman/Photo Edit, Inc. **H28** (t) ©Jim Steinberg/Photo Researchers, Inc. (tc) ©2001 Cynthia Malaran http://www. malaran.com from the websitehttp://www. watchingthechanges.com All Rights Reserved. (c) Joe McDonald/Corbis. (bc) ©Steve Skjold/Photo Edit, Inc. ASSIGNMENT: **H18** (b), **H21** (bc), **H25, H27** (bc), **H28** (bc)©HMco./Ken Karp Photography. **H18** (t), **H19–H21**, (b), **H22–H24, H27** ©HMco./Richard Hutchings Photography ILLUSTRATION: **H24** Patrick Gnan. **H26** Promotion Studios.

H35